Of Grief, Garlic and Gratitude

Praise for Of Grief, Garlic and Gratitude

Kris Francoeur's book is both heart-breaking and inspirational—heartbreaking because of the loss it recounts with such loving care, and inspiring because of the radical honesty with which the story is told.

—David Moats,
Winner of the Pulitzer Prize in Journalism

Kristin Francoeur's *Of Grief, Garlic, and Gratitude* is a deeply moving and articulate memoir of grief. It brought me to tears. This lovely book honors her 20 year old son Sam, whose untimely death launched this requiem about the complexity of grief. Kristin Francoeur honors Sam, his friends, her family, her community, but most of all, she honors her grief process. This book is a part of Sam's enduring legacy and a gift for each reader, since we all experience grief and loss. Kristin Francoeur has truly given meaning to her suffering and we are all the richer for it. *Of Grief, Garlic, and Gratitude* is a powerful narrative that is simultaneously personal and universal.

—Jack Mayer,
M.D., author of *Life in a Jar: The Irena Sendler Project* and *Before the Court of Heaven*

This book kept me it its grip from the beginning. Beautifully written, it took me through the rollercoaster emotions of the loss of a child: denial, anger, acceptance, love, joy and more. Creatively written as a daily, weekly, monthly, annual personal journal, I found it hard to put down, waiting for the story to keep unfolding. Author Francoeur's son Sam died accidentally from a drug overdose; however, the author's courage to tell this story gives us an awareness of the mental health and life challenges of a young man who lived and loved people relentlessly. This book is a gift.

—Tom Dutta,
#1 International Bestselling Author of *The Way of the Quiet Warrior™*,
Founder and CEO of KRE-AT

This book is a mother's heartfelt account of her struggle after losing her son. Sadly, parents across the country are dealing with this same devastating loss every single day. It is time as a nation to fully focus on preventing opioid addiction to the full extent possible and treating people with addiction with compassion and comprehensive therapy to stop the loss of our loved ones and avoid every parent's worst nightmare.

—Stephen Leffler,
M.D., Professor of Emergency Medicine UVM College of Medicine

I thought it would be too painful for me to read this book. It was painful, but not too painful. The balance of personal perspective, brutal honesty (including alerts to tirades and snarky comments), and lovely, happy times mixed among the unbearable grief kept me going. I wanted and needed to know how the author and family managed. For me, the highlights were the chronicles of how accepting, compassionate, nonjudgmental, and "bigger than life" Sam was. His passion for music, lyrics and theater are infectious. It was heart-warming and impressive to learn about all the people who emerged as supports and friends to bolster his family. The author's advice to parents who complain about their children's various foibles should be seriously taken to heart. I can now admit to why I kept every painting, story, spelling and writing assignment etc. that our children produced when they were young. One never knows…. Sharing and spreading love is perhaps the greatest lesson. Love changes and matures, but in the end, it endures.

—Dr. Johana Kashiwa Brakeley,
M.D., F.A.A.P., Pediatrician

Of Grief, Garlic and Gratitude

RETURNING TO HOPE & JOY FROM A SHATTERED LIFE

Sam's Love Story

—KRIS FRANCOEUR—

NEW YORK

LONDON • NASHVILLE • MELBOURNE • VANCOUVER

Of Grief, Garlic and Gratitude

Returning to Hope and Joy from a Shattered Life—Sam's Love Story

Published in New York, New York, by Morgan James Publishing. Morgan James is a trademark of Morgan James, LLC. www.MorganJamesPublishing.com

ISBN 9781642791815 paperback
ISBN 9781642791822 eBook
Library of Congress Control Number: 2018950359

Cover & Interior Design by:
Christopher Kirk
GFSstudio.com

In an effort to support local communities, raise awareness and funds, Morgan James Publishing donates a percentage of all book sales for the life of each book to Habitat for Humanity Peninsula and Greater Williamsburg.

Get involved today! Visit
www.MorganJamesBuilds.com

For Sam—your love and light guide me each day.
Thank you for choosing me be your mom, now and forever.

Table of Contents

The Why

There's no tragedy in life like the death of a child.
Things never get back to the way they were.
Dwight D. Eisenhower

How lucky I am to have something
that makes saying goodbye so hard.
Winnie the Pooh

The last time I saw him? Alive? He was walking away slowly, keeping pace with his Beepa, talking about his day, gesturing broadly, his voice ringing through the fall air, a huge smile on his face.

The last words? "I love you," said all around.

Those give me some small measure of peace, once in a while.

My life is divided into two parts by a glaringly clear line. The first part was anything before October 9, 2013, and the other, everything after. This book is about the after.

Before you read this, you must understand this is my story—not yours, or that of anyone in my family. Originally, I thought this would be Sam's story, but truly it isn't. Sam would have needed to tell his own story, and unfortunately, he won't ever be able to do that. This is my story of who Sam was/is for me, and my story of loving him, losing him, and my journey forward. It is the story of Sam's love, hence the subtitle of the book.

Dr. Jernstedt of Dartmouth College once said that educators must remember that a person's perception is their own reality. As you read this, please know that this is my perception, so therefore it is my reality. Some who have shared this journey with me may remember things or perceive them differently and may feel that I am not depicting things accurately. I never intended to misconstrue anything; this is how I perceive what has happened. Please also know that while there is some semblance of chronology to this story, as with any of us, at times memories pop up and they are included where they arose.

This also is the story of the use of social media in my life. While I used Facebook a bit prior to our loss, it somehow became a major means of communication after. I never intended to write posts for other people. As I struggled, I wrote for myself but needed to validate it somehow by posting online. While my original posts are included here, only some of the responses (with names redacted) are included, as again, this is my story. Some of the posts have been edited for length or redundancy, but no overall content or themes have been changed. Not all of my posts have been included here, some because they didn't fit the overall theme/goal of this book, or because they were echoes of what others had already said. Any names mentioned in this book were used with permission. Throughout the book are lyrics from songs by the group Twiddle, and those lyrics are used with permission. Finally, as you read Facebook posts, please know that any typos appear unedited, just as they were. If multiple posts were written on the same date, the date is noted at the start of the post.

As you read this, I would ask that you understand that from my point of view, losing a child is a different kind of loss from any other. No matter how much you love your parents, your spouse, your dog, you understand that there is a possibility that person or animal will pass before you—it is the order of the universe. In my opinion, and from having talked with many people who have experienced the death of a child or a spouse, it is my strong belief that the death of a child is a completely different sort of loss. Having said that, this is a book about how I've dealt with my loss, but I feel that both self-aware-ness and gratitude can help us in any sort of situation.

Finally, you must understand that part of my journey, the part that will not end until I am reunited with Sam, is the never-ending list of regrets. You should understand that the would-haves, could-haves, should-haves are mine, and mine alone—everyone in Sam's life has their own. You have no right to tell me that I should or shouldn't feel a certain way, just as I can't say that to others in Sam's life. Guilt is our own; we have to learn to live with it the best we can. On my good days, I can say that I did the best I could. On my bad days, the guilt is almost unbearable.

Why, if the journey has been that painful, did I write this book? When I started, I would have said I was writing it because so many people in my life—people I knew personally and even friends of friends—suggested that I put together the story of my continuing journey with my posts, in hopes that someone else might be helped by the ideas of conscious and deliberate expression of gratitude, connection with nature, and loving those around us. As time went on, I thought a lot about the fact that in my life as a professional writer, I write romance novels—you know, the happily-ever-after stories. But in my personal life, there isn't a true happily-ever-after; there instead is finding-joy-where-and-when-you-can. Now, as the book is completed, I realize that the "why" is that I feel it is my responsibility to be one of the many faces of the impact of the opiate addiction, while also pushing myself and those around me to find joy where they can, and to love as fiercely and openly as possible.

I am not perfect. I am not the perfect wife, mother, daughter, stepmother, daughter-in-law, employee, grandmother, housekeeper, cook, or farmer. This is not the story of an expert on handling grief or of someone formally schooled in the benefits of gratitude. It is not a guide to anything. Instead, it's the story of a fortysomething woman trying her best each day, trying to live with pur-pose, and trying to, as Twiddle would say, "love relentlessly," as Sam did.

Welcome to my journey.

CHAPTER ONE

October 9, 2013

And when you hear my final cry,
Well, I'll always be there in your soul.

Every Soul—Twiddle

On October 10, 2013, I posted the following one hundred words on Facebook. It took me almost an hour to write.

———

Thursday, October 10, 2013

It is with breaking hearts that we want to share with our family and friends that yesterday our beloved son Sam passed away. We were so blessed to have shared his life for more than 20 years, and can't count all the joyous and love-filled moments we shared with him. We ask for your understanding and patience right now, as we may not respond to messages, emails, texts or calls—but please understand that we so appreciate the outpouring of love. A celebration of his life will happen this Sunday at 1:00 p.m. at the Leicester Meeting House.

———

A day later, I was still in total shock. The day before, at exactly 5:34 a.m., our phone had rung. I know exactly what time it was because the phone is next to the alarm clock. Normally we would have been up by then, but I had just been diagnosed with diverticulitis, a painful digestive disorder, and was set to be home sick that day.

Seeing it was my parents' number, still half-asleep, I answered to hear my mother's voice. "Kristin, you need to come up here right now. They think Sam is dead."

At exactly 5:34 a.m. on October 9, 2013, our lives were irrevocably changed. We were shattered, our hearts broken.

Now, years later, I still can't let myself think a lot about that moment. It's like opening a door to a place so dark that I'm afraid if I go, I may never return. We later learned that the EMTs had pronounced Sam dead by the time she called, but in her own grief, my mother probably thought the kindest thing was to tell us they "thought" he might be gone. Maybe she wasn't thinking it through that clearly either; maybe it wasn't a planned choice of words. After all, how do you call your daughter to say that you've found her son—your grandson—dead?

How could this be happening to us? How? We'd seen Sam just the day before. I came home early from work because I had been so sick, and I picked him up from his intern job at the farm where he lived, and brought him home with me. We'd spent the afternoon watching *Law and Order.* Then he did chores for me, and proceeded to tell me my Brussels sprouts plants looked like crap. After my husband Paul came home, Sam decided to go with my parents to his brother Ben's soccer game at Otter Valley; he'd wanted to go see a couple of teachers when he was there. He still loved his high school teachers so much he often went back for regular visits. His mood was so good as he talked about who he wanted to see, and then we decided that we would go down toward the end of the game to pick Ben up, which we did.

That afternoon was perfect—sunny, not too hot. The foliage here in Vermont was spectacular. When we got there, Sam was sitting on the bleachers with my parents, his Mormor and Beepa, cheering for Ben at the top of his lungs like he always did. After the game, we all visited with Coach Muffie and her son Barron. Then Sam asked about coming home with us for the night instead of going back to the farm. I said he was always welcome to come home, but I didn't know what we'd have for dinner because I only had a little bit of frozen lasagna since I'd been feeling so lousy that I hadn't gotten groceries in quite a while. *Forever* I will live with the guilt that maybe if I'd had more lasagna, our lives would be different.

Knowing I was stressed about feeding everyone, my mom offered to have Sam stay at their house, less than a half-hour away from ours; that alleviated some of my guilt. At least then it did.

That night, Sam called. Rolling over to answer the phone, I saw it was 9:09. It's funny how your brain remembers details like that. Ben, Paul, and I were up in our room, watching something on TV but I don't remember what. Ben was stretched out in Paul's recliner and I was almost asleep in bed. The conversation was mundane—Sam told us what he had for dinner and said he was watching TV with my dad. Then he said, "Love you, Mom. I'll call you in the morning." That was nothing unusual; Sam called me at least three times a day, every day. With his words, I knew with certainty that he would call me mid-morning as he worked at the farmers' market. He then said he wanted to say goodnight to Paul and Ben, so I held the phone out as he yelled goodnight and said he loved them, and they yelled that they loved him too. One thing I'll forever be thankful for is that our last words to each other were words of love. Despite the many rocky moments in our last months with Sam as we dealt with his substance abuse, his poor choices that landed him in trouble with the law, and his struggle with his bipolar disorder, still, love was the strongest emotion.

So now we had received a call that Sam was "maybe" gone. We quickly got dressed, and woke Ben up to tell him we had to go to my parents' house, but we wanted him to stay home from school. We didn't tell him the reason, and although I've never asked him again what he thought—too dark a place to go—I assume he thought something had happened to one of my parents. We called Paul's parents, who live next door, to stay with Ben (again, not saying why we had to go out at such an ungodly hour) and drove as fast as we could to my parents' house, praying that Sam would be okay, willing ourselves to get there in time. If we could get there while he was still alive, maybe we could save him with sheer force of will—with just the depth of our love.

Later, at least days if not longer, Paul and I would talk about realizing that Sam was truly dead because as soon as we got to the village of Ripton, we saw that the ambulance didn't have its lights on as it sat in my parents' driveway, and when we pulled up, the EMTs were already packing their equipment back in the ambulance. If there was any hope to save him, they wouldn't have been packing up so soon.

Even now I can't write about that next hour without crying, without my chest clenching, my throat gripped with grief—I can't even swallow as I read those words, let alone when I wrote them for the first time.

No parent should ever see their child dead. Period. That goes against everything that seems right and logical in the universe; it's just not the natural order of things. Think back to that incredible moment when you saw your child for the first time, that absolute rush of emotion, of love, in those first few minutes. But helplessly seeing your child lie lifeless? It is that same strength of emotion, but pain, and exponentially larger.

The first hour or so after we arrived was absolute agony. We went into the house, to an addition Paul had built for my parents, and found our beautiful, loud, loving, hysterically funny, irreverent, sometimes grubby son lying dead on their floor, dressed in a sweater and sweatpants he'd borrowed from my dad because (of no surprise to anyone who knew him) he'd forgotten to bring pajamas. I remember keening; I'd never understood what that meant, and it wasn't a conscious decision like, "Gosh, I think I'll keen now." The pain of seeing him there, and realizing he was gone, was so agonizing that all I could do was rock in a near-fetal position, clutching Paul as we held Sam's cold body. I couldn't breathe. My lungs were so tight with the pain that I was close to hyperventilating. In the years since, I've consistently struggled with lung/breathing issues, which I never had prior to his death. Maybe the pain permanently tightened my chest? No matter—it's never gone away. In my heart, no matter the medications and inhalers, I don't think my chest will ever fully relax until I hold Sam in my arms again.

Then we realized that besides the EMTs, there was a State Police investigator and a representative from the Medical Examiner's office, so we all introduced ourselves. I don't actually know what we did after that for a while, as that time is completely blank in my memory. It's all just this horrible, painful blur.

About 90 minutes after we arrived, we asked the medical examiner for the cause of death. Sam had substance abuse issues and also struggled with his mental health. Was it "just" an overdose? Was it a medical fluke? Was it suicide? We waited for her response, knowing no matter what she said, the outcome was the same. She told us that while she couldn't make an official determination without an autopsy, she was tentatively ruling out suicide.

Again, on the list of things no parent should ever have to hear: your child will be autopsied.

You are supposed to hear that your child is going to college, getting married, having children, buying a house—anything but being dissected on a cold steel table. Not that I had ever seen an actual autopsy, but I'd watched enough crime shows to have a pop culture sense of what would happen, and that should never, ever happen to your child. Never. Just writing the word "autopsy" still makes me queasy. Even now, years after that hellish day, hearing the word itself makes little white lights dance around the edges of my visual field, and dizziness pushes at me as I swallow to keep the bile down.

Somehow I was sitting on my parents' couch. This slightly faded blue-and-white checked couch, a place Sam had slept many times when he'd stayed over. For some reason, one of my parents handed me the pants Sam had been wearing the night before. Maybe they handed them to me because they too needed something to do with their hands. Maybe they were in the way where they wanted to sit—I don't know. All I know is that this faded, stained pair of work pants, still smelling slightly of the earth, was now in my hands. I went through the pockets (both out of habit and the need to do something with my freezing cold hands) and I found the wrapper of a pain medication my dad had been taking.

And we knew.

Before you start thinking this is the story of a suicide, it isn't.

If it was, I'd say so. The end result was the same, but it wasn't intentional.

This was a case of an accidental drug overdose. We all knew of Sam's issues and my parents had locked up every possible medication in the house except this one because none of us knew it could be a problem.

Side rant: perhaps the first of many. Turns out there had been three—count them—*three* deaths from fentanyl (patches and otherwise) in our little county in the six weeks before Sam's death, but that had been kept out of the press because Addison County didn't want to recognize—or be recognized for—a growing opiate problem. We didn't know that the medication could be abused, so it was the only drug that hadn't been locked up. The need for the towns surrounding Middlebury, Vermont, and Middlebury College in particular to keep their pure, healthy, never-do-anything-wrong image meant that they withheld information from the public. And now, partially because of this, Sam was dead.

I handed the wrapper of the transdermal pain patch to the M.E. and she walked over to Sam's body, still lying on the floor. The medical examiner was still there because she was waiting for the funeral home to arrive to take his body away. With a gloved finger, she gently reached into his mouth and pulled a patch from inside his cheek, the cause of death now immediately apparent. Over the next couple of months, we would learn that such pain patches are often abused in this way: there is an immediate high experienced when put in the mouth, and in Sam's case, immediate death.

So, there we were, talking with the State Police investigator for almost two hours, filling the time until the hearse got there. This was a complete stranger, but the silence was so heavy that we started making mindless conversation. Clearly trying to find something neutral to talk about, he mentioned that his daughter had been in theater with our boys. Theater? The investigator's daughter was in theater with Sam and Ben? Wow.

Theater is a big deal in our household—a *huge* deal, especially for Sam and Ben, and they had a huge circle of friends from high school theater all across Vermont. With his comment, we realized that as soon as it went out over the scanner that a 20-year-old had died at that address in Ripton, people would put everything together and soon all of Addison County would know that Sam was dead, when the rest of our children knew nothing, nor did anyone else outside of that room. We were well-known in the community, so it would be big news. Within minutes, we were requesting that the police delay relaying the details over the scanner until we could tell our children; they deserved to know before the rest of the world.

Every minute, Paul and I were holding onto each other with absolute death grips (I know, bad choice of words). As I look back now, I can remember doing some very specific things, and then there are blocks of time I can't account for. Once we arranged for the news to be held back a bit, we knew we needed to get home to Ben.

But then we would be leaving Sam's body there.

To decide whether to stay with the body of your dead child or go home to be with his little brother was an almost unbearable decision. Leave or stay? How do you decide that? Stop for a moment as you read this and think about that decision. Leave? Stay? What would you do?

Finally, we decided that Ben had to be terrified, and we needed to go to him. I asked my dad, who also happened to be a minister, if he would sit with Sam's body until the undertaker arrived, and asked him if he would perform some sort of last rites, knowing that the Catholic relatives would want that. With tears running down his wrinkled cheeks, he promised me he would, and that he wouldn't leave Sam alone in that time. Thinking back now, I have never asked my dad what he did as he sat with him, other than the prayers. Did he talk to Sam? Did he pray? Did he hold his hands or stroke his hair? What did he do?

Then I asked the medical examiner if I could take some of Sam's hair. I don't know why, but I wanted it, so she helped me cut some. The funny thing is, she seemed to think nothing of it; as if it wasn't an unusual request. Maybe it wasn't; I don't know.

Then we said goodbye to our beautiful baby and lovingly draped an afghan over him as if to keep him warm. We held his body one final time, held his hands, stroked his face, touched his scruffy beard, and kissed his cheeks once more, realizing that was the last time we would physically see him in this lifetime.

At one point, a friend had posted on Facebook that there was nothing harder than leaving your child at college. Let me tell you, dropping your child off to college and saying that goodbye is hard, and yes, I cried each time we did it. But saying goodbye to your child *forever*? *That* is hard—make no mistake about the difference.

We drove home in silence, in shock, dreading what we had to do. We arrived home and found fifteen year-old Ben alone; he'd told Paul's parents that he was fine and could stay by himself. Paul and I sat on the living room coffee table facing Ben on the couch, him lying there under his favorite blanket, and we told him. That will forever be one of the hardest things I have ever done, and again, a door I can't open because even typing the words now takes my breath away.

Our four kids love each other with ferocious devotion. That's not to say they don't fight or get on each other's nerves. But their loyalty to each other is legendary—God help anyone who messed with one of them, because you got the entire group in response. Everyone in our local community knew that, and people talked about it all the time. They talked about it partially because everyone knew that they aren't full biological siblings, and there is almost sixteen years difference in age between Amie (Paul's oldest) and Ben (our youngest). Sam and Ben are full siblings, while Amie and Ryan are Paul's children from a previous marriage. Sam was the glue between the two sets of kids, and his connection to his siblings was deeper than I can express. Sam looked up to Amie and Ryan, believed in them, worshiped them. But Ben? Sam protected Ben, encouraged him, irritated him, pushed him to greatness, and made fun of him. He was Ben's hero and best friend. Telling Ben he was gone was hell.

By now it was mid-to-late morning, and Paul went to tell his parents. Then we repeatedly called Amie, who was pregnant with her first child, but we couldn't reach her as she was taking a graduate class. So we also kept calling her wife, and couldn't reach her either. We tried to reach our oldest son, Ryan, who was living in New Hampshire in an area without cell service. So, we kept calling the three, leaving messages to call us. Leaving no specifics, we just said that we needed them to call us immediately. Finally we reached both Amie and Ryan, and told them. The shock in their voices, the pain? It was so hard to hear, just unbearable.

Then Paul stayed with Ben, sitting with him in silence as they watched something mundane on television, while I called the mother of Sam's best friend, asking her to tell her son who was in Boston. Through her sobs, she said she would get in the car and drive down to tell him because she couldn't bear the thought of him being alone when he heard the news. We called our neighbor so he could tell his daughter, who'd been one of Sam's closest friends since kindergarten. Within minutes, their family was in our hallway, sobbing with us. We called our friend Leah to get a hold of her daughter, Linnea, one of Sam's dearest friends and one of the loves of his life, who was studying in Bhutan.

In the midst of all of these calls, my cell phone rang. It was Hannah, our former daughter-in-law and Sam's employer. I answered the phone, and before I could say anything, she said, "Kris, it's Hannah. Is Sam there? He's supposed to be at farmers' market with me."

That was the first of many phone calls that would rip my heart out. She was calling because he was late for work. It wouldn't have been the first time he was late for work. I had gotten calls like this from Hannah before. I would have promised her I would find him and get him there as fast as I could. Instead, I told her of our new reality. Hannah isn't someone you normally would expect to cry, but she started to sob, then hung up.

Then we called Otter Valley Union High School and told our friend Meredith, who had been both Sam's and Ben's guidance counselor, and together with her, we figured out how Otter Valley would be made aware. If you don't live in small town Vermont, then you should know that especially when you've lived in an area for decades, raised four "memorable" kids who all went to the same high school, everyone is connected to each other in some way. It's like *Six Degrees of Separation* on a much bigger scale—*everyone* is connected. In the case of calling Otter Valley, our kids were very well-known and well-loved there, and in particular, Sam had been a near-legendary character in that school for his six years (middle and high school) and stayed connected after he'd graduated.

The reality was, at least in regard to Otter Valley, that Sam was larger than life, louder than loud. He saw every moment as an opportunity for something really cool to happen, and people responded to that, even when his exuberance was irritating. *Everyone* knew Sam; he went out of his way to know everyone. A new teacher arrived? He'd go introduce himself. Seventh graders started school, terrified of being in the "big" school? Sam invited them to eat at his lunch table. The weird Goth kid who everyone stayed away from? Sam struck up a conversation about music. He knew every single adult and student in the building, and even with everyone knowing of the struggles he'd had, he was loved beyond belief because he loved every single person. So we called Otter Valley, knowing that the news of his death would have a significant impact on the school community.

Realizing that I was going to need to be out of work for a bit, I called my boss (who was out) and instead got through to the assistant superintendent. No one tells you how many stinking phone calls you have to make when someone dies, or how important the order of the calls is. It's pure agony—

you keep dialing the phone, keep saying those awful words, keep having to tell the story, keep having to hear the heartbreak in others and do your best to console them when your own heart is barely beating through the sheer pain of it all.

At 2:15 that afternoon, Otter Valley canceled theater rehearsal for the day. Theater practices *never* get canceled, so the theater kids knew something major had happened. At 2:30, there was a faculty meeting where Sam's death was announced to the staff and by 2:32, as we were on the phone with a good friend, she got a text from her son that kids were getting the news via text and Facebook on the buses, and it was spreading faster and wider than we could have ever imagined.

At 3:00, Paul and I had an appointment at the funeral home. Remember, we are talking about a small town; our daughter had dated the funeral director's son in high school, so we'd known each other a long time. There we were, still so shocked that we couldn't even take a deep breath, trying to make arrangements. We sat in velvet chairs, while Gary, the funeral director, asked us questions.

What did we want for a funeral service? A private one; this hurt too much to have it on public display. We wanted a teeny-tiny family service where no one else would see how incredibly broken we were.

In his gentle, soothing voice, he asked us to reconsider as he reminded us how many people loved Sam and would want the opportunity to honor him with us. Haltingly and somewhat begrudgingly, we agreed to have a small service at the town meeting hall; Paul and I had been married there and our children had all performed in Leicester School events. Just a small service, we thought, not expecting many people outside of family, but anyone was welcome and my father would do the service. My father—my elderly father—would perform the service for the grandson who was one of the absolute lights of his life.

The questions went on: Did we want to bury him in a casket or cremate him?

Cremation or burial? How? How could we be asked that? Just the day before I'd been talking with Sam about how excited he was about his new job at the Middlebury College Snow Bowl ski area. Now, almost exactly 24 hours later, we were being asked whether we wanted to have his beautiful body rot in a wooden box or reduce him to ashes. The decision for cremation was mutual. I don't know why cremation seemed better to me, but it did in that moment and still does now.

Gary went on to ask what kind of urn we wanted.

An urn?

An urn.

We were going to make a decision about what to put his remains in. If he was being cremated, we had to decide where his ashes would be stored. Repeatedly swallowing hard to keep from vomiting, we said we needed to think about it, and he told us we could look at different options once we finished other details.

The questions continued. Did we want flowers for the service?

Are you freaking kidding me? This was a kid who only had a corsage for his prom date because I ordered it and picked it up.

Flowers?

Yeah, we really wanted those great big hideous gladiolas to grace the table next to the urn with his ashes, I thought as I secretly rolled my eyes.

No, we didn't want donations of flowers. Gaudy flowers were not Sam. Sam was garlic, squash, hot peppers, and LEGO bricks—not fancy flowers. Requests for memorial donations to Otter Valley's theater program seemed more apropos.

Music?

Did we want to have a musician at the service?

No. Sam loved music. Classical, rap, punk, indie—he loved it all. But a professional musician playing funeral music? Not on your life. We would ask Sam's best friend Will to play a piece on the piano, and then have CDs of other selections. We decided we would ask his friends and our families for songs that meant a lot to Sam, and those would be what we would play.

Speeches?

We would tell friends and family ahead of time that anyone who wanted to speak, could. Suddenly, I felt as if I wanted to say a few words myself. Paul said he didn't know if he could do it, but he would stand with me for support.

Food? A reception?

No, there would be no party after the service. Receptions are for *joy*. In my mind, I couldn't stand the thought of having to sit around a table and try to eat after my son's funeral service.

Again, so gently, as if he were talking to a terrified, cornered animal, Gary suggested some sort of refreshments after the service. What about cookies? Maybe brownies and cider?

We could do that. Sam loved sweets, especially cookies, and always claimed the center square of a pan of brownies and washed them down with a lot of cider (preferably that he'd made with his dad). We could do cider, brownies, and cookies. Gary suggested that the community wanted to help, so if we asked, people would bring the snacks.

Program? We would make one as a family, and Gary would make copies.

Photos? Yes, we would find photos. We would ask the community to send us photos, and we would make displays of the joy and wonder that was Sam.

Ponies? Balloons? A band? No, not really, but the questions felt that numerous. Lucky for us, Gary knew our whole family so he was able to offer more guidance than most people probably get.

Finally, when it couldn't be avoided any longer, we had to look at urns. Nothing in your life can prepare you for the hell of picking out an urn for your beloved child. This larger-than-life ox of a boy—tall, strong, noisy, with huge feet—was going to fit into one of those small containers.

I remember taking a mint from Gary's bowl, sucking on it feverishly, my mouth so dry the candy wasn't even dissolving as I tried to keep breathing. There were so many moments in that meeting that I thought I was going to pass out. Urns, urns, urns, next to caskets; my sneakered feet sinking into the plush carpet of the showroom with all these elaborately morbid trappings.

How could this be happening? Sam was set to move into a new apartment on October 15th; we had just bought him a new comforter for his bed there. Now we were looking at these shiny, gaudy urns in which to store his earthly remains? *No, no, no, no! This could not be happening.*

There was no way we could choose anything they had; they weren't him. This was a boy whose favorite shoes were baby blue Crocs; his favorite shirts were faded flannel; he wanted to have a room dedicated to his Lego sets in his new apartment. How could we put his remains in a shiny metallic urn or some fancy ceramic vessel? Paul asked if perhaps there was a simple wooden model, and thankfully Gary found one in the back room, needing to be dusted off as he brought it out to us. Even in our pain, we looked at it in awe. It was a beautiful box: simple carved wood, like something Sam would have picked for a treasure box.

We started on the obituary. Again, luckily Gary knew us, because he helped us with remembering important details. We were in such shock, we couldn't think of what to include. How do you reduce such a life to a couple of paragraphs? Slowly, Gary led us each step of the way. He knew we had traveled a lot as a family, so he asked us about travel memories, which we shared through our tears, especially the memories of our trips to London, Mexico, and places we had gone to see the Red Sox play. He knew Sam loved Legos so he asked about that. He even remembered that Sam had a special cat, so she could be mentioned in the obituary. Gary helped us recall important details that we were too shell-shocked to remember for ourselves.

Then there was the matter of a burial spot for his ashes (or most of them anyway). How many of you have your children's gravesites picked out ahead of time? Or even your own resting place?

We were at a complete loss—couldn't think of a place to bury him. We were in such a fog of shock and pain, we couldn't think of a single cemetery anywhere near our home—not one. Gary quietly suggested we think about the town cemetery at the bend in the road, right across the street from an alpaca farm.

That was a perfect place, a place Sam had loved going to every Memorial Day with Leicester School when they would walk down to honor veterans buried there. Gary would take care of calling the town to get a plot for Sam. Before we finally left his office an hour and a half later, we made an appointment to finish the final details the following day.

Now it was about 4:30; we'd been up since 5:34 a.m. We hadn't had anything to eat or drink all day, and we knew that there was nothing in the fridge because we still needed to shop. It's funny that I remember I was wearing a hoodie sweatshirt that day, one from our spinning wheel business. It was pretty warm that afternoon, but I was so overwhelmed that I was shivering with chills.

We went to the grocery store on our way home. Since the call at 5:34 that morning, unless we were using the bathroom, Paul and I had not stopped holding each other in some way. We had reached a point of such profound pain that I don't think we even spoke to each other as we shopped. I remember choosing a few apples thinking we needed to eat some fruit, then we went to the deli where I ordered turkey—a pound of roast turkey. Before we knew it, the young man waiting on us approached us from around the counter.

"You're Sam's parents, aren't you?" I'm sure we looked at him blankly; I don't think we could've recognized *anyone* right then. "I'm Cody, Sam's friend. I'm so, so sorry."

This beautiful young man was the first non-death professional that we'd seen in person, and he had the strength to come out and see us. He hugged us, cried with us, and then handed me the turkey with a "paid" sticker on it, saying it was the only thing he could think of to do to help. That simple gesture still makes my eyes fill with tears.

At home, Ben was lying in our bed under the covers, watching a rerun of the Red Sox game from the night before. Paul's parents were sitting downstairs, respecting his need for solitude. After giving them the updates on the details, and calling my parents with the information, we decided to order grinders.

Back to town we went. I remember going in to get the sandwiches at the pizza place, and thinking how weird it was that no one in the restaurant knew that Sam was gone yet. Our lives had been shattered, and yet all seemed so normal there. I was both relieved to not have to talk about it, and so angry that everyone there seemed so happy, so normal.

As I turned to go after paying, the cashier, this really wonderful kid, said, "Have a good night, Kris." I didn't know what to say, so I just said, "You too." How weird is it when you're falling apart but you still automatically exercise good manners? I guess I did actually listen to my mother's lectures over the years.

We got the grinders and took them to Branbury State Park on Lake Dunmore, one of our favorite family spots, and ate them in almost complete silence. After finishing his sandwich, Ben stood up without a word, walked into the shimmering lake, and dove into the water, still in his clothes. Paul and I sat on the retaining wall at the beach, watching him, not saying a word, tears running down our cheeks unnoticed. Ben came out of the water, soaked, looking so sad and lost, before he started to shiver. Thankfully we always had towels and blankets in the car since our children often did things like jump in lakes, or he would've had a very wet ride home.

Later at home, we talked to Amie and Ryan again by phone. By this point, we'd talked to them at least three times since we'd delivered the news; now the phone conversations were more about checking in on details and needing to hear each other's voices. They were both set to arrive the next morning. Ryan would stay with us through the funeral at least, and Amie and Jen would go home to Burlington at night, but would come down each day.

The three of us watched *Titanic* that night. I don't think we said more than a hundred words the whole evening. We just all cried silently, shaking, holding on to each other and trying to process what was happening to us all. The three of us worked to make a bed for Ben on the floor of our room, needing to be together. As we finally shut off the television and turned off the lights, we all huddled under our blankets, tears still streaming, exhausted but too sad to sleep. I know what I was thinking then, and I suspect it was the same as Paul and Ben. *How could our lives have come to this? How could someone so alive, so much a part of the very fabric of our existence, be gone?*

CHAPTER TWO

The First Responses

The next morning, I awoke long before the alarm and lay there in bed, the tears starting before I even opened my eyes; my eyes already burning from being so swollen from the tears the day before. I lay there, processing the reality. Was it really true? Could it all just be a dream? Could I open the bedroom door like so many hundreds of times before, and find Sam sound asleep on the couch, snoring, the TV still on as he'd fallen asleep watching something? No, the reality slammed into me like a freight train and I felt myself fighting to breathe.

Later that day, I had to post *those words* on Facebook. Posting on social media when your child gets accepted to college, gets engaged, scores a home run, or gets the lead in a play? Those are all posts you like to write. Letting the world know that your child has died? You can't imagine a worse thing unless you've done it, but in this day of social media, it felt as if there was little choice.

As the news spread through phone calls, personal visits, and text messages, our phone rang and rang, people showed up at our door, kids walked into the house without knocking as they had done so many times before—Sam had brought his friends home day and night, and even in death, they just kept coming. But there were people in our lives who might not have heard the news through the "normal channels," so it was with shaking hands that I carefully chose the words.

Within minutes, responses started pouring in. What we didn't know was that Sam's own page was simultaneously filling with comments as well: an outpouring of grief from people around the world who loved him as much as he loved them.

I read the comments as they were posted to my page, knowing people were sending us their love, but the pain was so great I couldn't feel it. While there were hundreds of comments posted, these were the ones that I have looked at over and over again:

Oh my god, Kris. I am so, so sad—just devastated for you to hear this. Oh my friend, I am holding you and your family in my heart, in prayer, in love. I am so, so sorry.

Thinking of you all. Remembering all of the wonderful stories and pictures of Sam that you have shared over the years. Sending love and prayers your way.

I'm so sorry for your loss. You're in my thoughts. You're living a parents' worst nightmare and I wish I could do something to help.

{{{{{{HUGS}}}}}} I'm so sorry for your loss. {{{{{{{{HUGS}}}}}}}}

I can't even begin to understand your loss Kris. Our family is sending love and peace your way. He was a beautiful boy.

Kris, Paul, I know there's nothing I can say, but I'm saying it anyway with all my heart. Hold tightly to each other and know that Sam was as blessed to have you as you were to have him.

Love and, when it can come, peace—to you, Kris, and all your family. We are thinking of you.

My dear friend,

The inexpressible sadness—words fail me. Our hearts ache for you and Paul and young Ben.

Beautiful Boy

My parents lost two of their children and I became their only child. The grief goes very deep and never goes completely away but somehow we managed to muddle through and come out willing to move forward in a positive direction. May your pain slowly be lessened as you move through the grieving process, remembering the joy and love you had in Sam.

Meanwhile, Sam's page was also filling with posts, some included here, and pictures, showing the deep love he had inspired and shared. While this is my story, I am including some of them as they highlight who Sam is to *me*, and to help show how others viewed him.

Love you Sam. You were one of the kindest, happiest, easiest going persons and many people will be hurt by your leaving.

You were the funniest person I have ever met. :(I'm gonna miss you.

"Life ain't always beautiful, sometimes it's just plain hard. Life can knock you down, it can break your heart"—Rest in the sweetest peace. You will be missed beyond words.

The world will miss the smile that you greeted it with every day.

He was a good man who had a rough path but a beautiful heart.

That was one of my favorite posts, because it was so very true. Sam's heart was pure beauty, and his path had not always been easy.

You stood out from the rest when you said "I ain't ever gonna learn this sh%#" when I was teaching you choreography for Joseph. Rest in peace bud.

Infinite love.

Sam will make her dance. Sam will make her dance. Twiddle twiddle twiddle twiddle

---

I remember when I first met Sam in 7th grade home room and thought he was the biggest tool ever. Then I got to know him and realized he was one of the funniest and most insightful people I ever met.

I never saw you in a bad mood, if there was conflict you were there to say something like "hey guys let's just hug it out instead" always making someone laugh!!

I remember coming to OV and you were one of the first people to introduce yourself to me. I admired your individual spirit and your sense of humor. High school wasn't easy and I'm glad you took an interest in me. You are an amazing soul.

You were an inspiration to me as a young actor. Seeing you on stage made me think that I wanted to be right up there with you.

The first time I met Sam was back in middle school, riding the late bus. He came over and sat across from me and proceeded to crack jokes and make me laugh the entire ride home. Sam continued to spend the rest of his life, just as he did that day, going out of his way to make people smile and laugh.

You were good friends with my brother and we became friends too. I remember we built a toy car out of Legos in 2nd grade, living life the way kids should. You were always right down the road and were always so friendly, just a true genuine person.

"EVEN IN THE STEW OF SOCIETY EVEN THE SCUM RISES TO THE TOP!!" From harmonizing West Virginia to running from the ice caves in the biggest storm I've ever seen... the man, the beard, Samuel.

I'm willing to endure the embarrassment of this pubescent gem again because this is still brilliant. Love you [A YouTube link was included here in the post. Please google YouTube—this is NOT a fungus to see the video.]

That YouTube link? It was a science project Sam did with some friends in high school, and it is such a beautiful example of his love, joy, and sense of humor.

Back to the Facebook posts:

To a guy who was always the light of the room and could brighten up anyone's day with a joke and a wide smile. Rest in peace, you will be missed by many.

You were always ready with a smile or a joke to brighten someone's day, all I can say is you will be missed.

I'll eat a whole pizza, a sleeve of Oreos—watch a movie, chill and screw the test I have tomorrow, that's what he would have wanted— love you "Captain" Samuel M. Francoeur.

"Captain" Samuel Francoeur... When Sam was graduating from Otter Valley, he had to go to a week's worth of graduation practices. He had a real dislike of ridiculous rituals, so spending a week practicing walking in and out of the gym was not something he did graciously. He was a pain in the rear end during that week. He arrived late, made people laugh, tried to show that he felt this was not necessary. There was a teacher who ran the graduation practices year after year, with absolute dedication to the process. When she called Sam's name in the practice of accepting the diplomas, he'd loudly quip, "That's *Captain* Samuel Francoeur, if you please." On his graduation day, as his dear friend and class president read the names of each of the graduates, she looked at Sam with a sparkle in her eyes (you could see that the kids knew something was going to happen) and she proudly announced, "Captain Samuel M. Francoeur," causing a roar of approval from his friends. That was Sam. He livened up any event, no matter how trivial and mundane it was.

Certainly one of the funnier people I have come across in my days. We won't forget ya lobstaaaaa boyy.

Ah, the lobster boy. In one of Sam's many plays with Otter Valley's Walking Stick Theater group, he played a part where he was the lobster boy. He wore these god-awful Daisy Duke shorts, fishnet stockings, and lobster claw gloves. The name stuck for a long, long time.

No words could comprehend the amount of love this kid had for everyone. <3 RIP

Can't wait to run from lighting with you again someday.

I can't even begin to try and tally up the endless "heyyy buddddyyys" you've said to me, the awkward waves you've shot my way, the deep intellectual conversations, the very not so deep intellectual conversations, the hugs, and of course the laughs we've shared. Seems like just yesterday we were sitting in the back of theater talking about women, aliens, and the occasional bank heist. You'll always be in our hearts buddy, and never far from our thoughts. Rest in peace Sam Francoeur.

Bank heists. Sam got these ideas stuck in his head, and would bring them up over and over. There was a very famous armored truck robbery that occurred in Rutland, VT many years ago. Sam had spent countless hours trying to figure out how they'd done it (and gotten away with it) and he loved to watch movies like *The Italian Job*, so you could be sitting in a nice restaurant and all of a sudden, he'd bring up the subject of bank heists in a very hypothetical way.

I'll miss you constantly trying to lick my face. But more importantly, I'll miss you.

I'll let Twiddle do the talking...
"We'll meet again someday
You smile and then I'll say
When it rains it pours all day"
I know you are dancing to twiddle up in heaven.

The summer before my senior year of high school, Sam and I shared a grand adventure bushwhacking through the woods in the middle of the night at my first and only Solar Fest, totally lost and refusing to turn around until we got bogged down in knee-deep mud. I've only made a few insta-friends like that in my lifetime, and I'm really happy to say that Sam was one of them. Running into him on campus was like teleporting to that summer day, smile as bright as the sun in your eyes. A vibrant soul like that will easily live on in our stories and memories. What a guy!

Yesterday, many others and myself lost a great person in our lives. Sam was a terrific person and a great friend to many. Just in the short amount of time I knew him, I knew there was no one else like him. No one that even came close to being like him. I'm glad that I got to meet and become friends with him, I just wish mine and Z's son would get the chance to meet his Uncle Sam. But I promise he will know who you were and know you were a part of this family.

That last post ripped the little part of my heart that was still beating right out of my chest. I knew immediately who wrote it without even looking at the name, and it made me think of two completely different incidents that occurred with Sam's friend, Z. Both of them show a piece of Sam.

The first incident that post made me think of was in the early spring of Sam's senior year. Sam's friend Z was taken from his mother by the state, and he endured a horrible foster/adoptive home before disappearing for a while. We all knew that Sam and his friends were still in contact with him, but they wouldn't say where he was.

So again one afternoon I was at work, and Sam's high school principal called me. He was in his office with the boy's adoptive mother, representatives from the State Police and the Department of Children and Families, a guidance counselor, and Sam. All of the adults wanted to know where Z. was, and they knew that Sam knew, but he was refusing to tell them anything. Could I please get Sam to tell them, the principal asked. Once I finished clarifying that the principal was never, *ever* again to bring our child into a police matter without us being there, I told him to put Sam on the phone, and ask the adults to leave the room so I could talk to my son privately.

His voice was subdued. "Hi, Mom."

"Hey, Sammy."

I could hear him take a deep breath, then he almost whispered, "Are you going to tell me I have to tell?"

"Do you know where he is?"

His answer was quick. "Yes."

"Is he safe?"

"Yes."

"Will you tell me where he is?"

Sam's voice broke. "Mom, if you tell me I have to tell you, or them, I will. But I'm asking you to trust me. He's safe; he's okay; we can reach him. Please don't make me tell them. Please. Trust me."

Here I was, an assistant principal myself, knowing that my child knew where a minor was hiding, and yet, I trusted Sam's instincts. "I'll take care of this."

The principal got back on the phone and I told him that Sam assured me the friend was safe, and that he wasn't going to tell them anything more, and that we supported him in that, and that he was to immediately be returned to class. And he was.

That was Sam. He had his own code of honor. This friend's life had been awful, and he was now safe and happy, and Sam wasn't going to tell the inflictors of that pain how they could find him.

The second incident involving Z occurred a few weeks before Sam's graduation from high school. I was at work, doing the normal work stuff, and my assistant said I had a call. She said it was Jim, the principal at Otter Valley, but that it wasn't an emergency; he just needed to talk to me. So, I got on the phone, not sure how much heartburn this call was going to give me, and he calmly said, "Kris, do you guys have a sheep?"

What a strange question! "Yes."

"Does he like Hendrix?"

I certainly hadn't heard him correctly. "What?"

"Does your sheep like Jimi Hendrix?"

"Jim, what are you talking about?" Okay, the original conversation did have an expletive in it, but back to the story…

Now I could hear his suppressed laughter. "I think your sheep is outside the school, belted into the backseat of a Honda Civic, with Hendrix blasting. He's with Sam and the boys, and they are here to pick someone up."

I started to laugh, and even now, thinking back to the conversation, I laugh. "Seriously?"

"Yup."

So, I called Sam and when he answered, sure enough, Hendrix was blaring through the speakers. "Sam. Do you have Ferdie with you?" (Our ram's name was Ferdinand.)

"Hi, Mom." There was a chorus of "Hi, Moms" in the background and the bleating of a sheep. "Yeah, he's right here." And then he continued, "He's with me, Z, and the guys."

Sigh. "Sam, *why* is Ferdie at Otter Valley?"

His voice was patient. "Mom, he was *bored*. We went to the house to play basketball." Okay, he would've been skipping class to do that… Mental note to chew him out about that later. "We let him out to play with us, and he seemed bored, so we took him for a ride."

The funny thing was that it actually sounded pretty reasonable when explained in such a way. Wait, no, think about it. I swallowed and took a deep breath, "So, Sam, here's the deal. Turn down the music, get out of Otter Valley's circle, and take the sheep home. Got it?"

"Got it. Love you, Mom."

That was Sam's sense of logic, his ability to think differently than anyone else. In his mind, taking the ram for a ride on a beautiful spring day was a completely logical thing to do.

The Facebook posts continued:

Flying out tomorrow, I'll be there Sam.

They came in numbers we would never have expected. They drove, rode buses, carpooled, flew, hitchhiked, and in some cases, walked or biked, but they all showed up in the general area, all to show their love for Sam, and to honor him. That particular message was from a friend flying from halfway across the country, who called us and simply stated through his tears, "Paul, Kris, I'm flying out. I'll be there," and hung up (thankfully we recognized his voice).

Just remember as long as we are all here there's no reason not to let your legs dangle over the edge and giggle in the abyss. Love you forever, you were one smiley dude.

I lost the best friend I have ever known today. Sam, I love you more than words can express. With you, there was no judgment, only an ear to listen. Rest easy, baby. Let's hope all the other angels can keep up with you (though, I know they can't). XOXO.

"When it's time to shut your eyes, inside there's light that gives me life, to blind to see, so pure, so free, the love you gave to those in need, well I'm here my friend, this love won't end I'll spread your

word, no I won't turn back when times cut short and all that's left is your sweet love"—Twiddle

---

In theater you helped me learn how to be confident at being myself.

These posts showed me things I didn't know about Sam, things I continue to mull over even now. As a parent, you know who your child is to you, but you don't often get to see who your child is to *others*. I've learned about how his humor often defused tense situations, how he encouraged young actors to take risks, how he listened to anyone about anything without any judgment. Sam wasn't just our baby, our beloved son; he was so much to so many other people and it wasn't until he died that I truly got to see how important he was to such an astounding number of people.

Over the next weeks, months, years, more posts have been added to Sam's page, as people needed to leave visible messages to him and to others who miss him. Some of them get mentioned later on, but all have been left with love and the searing pain of loss.

CHAPTER THREE

Who am I? Who is Sam?

So, who am I? Why does it matter what I thought, or what I think? And who is Samuel Francoeur?

Prior to October 9, 2013, I would've told you that I was the only child of Wayne and Ellie, wife of Paul, mother (or stepmother, depending who is describing me) to Amie and Ryan, and mother to Sam and Ben. I was the assistant principal and support services administrator at a middle school in the second largest city in Vermont.

How did I become Paul's wife and the mother of his children? In 1991, the teachers at Leicester Central School noticed a nice single dad, who was often at school events for his very young daughter, Amie. They started plotting, and I started going to school functions to see this guy Paul, even though I was still in my final year of college. In September of 1991, we moved in together, thrusting me into instant parenthood with Amie and Ryan, who lived with Paul full-time. In May of 1992, we got married, and spent our wedding night in a Howard Johnson's with the two kids, ultimately sleeping in separate beds from one another because Amie and Ryan were kicking each other so badly that they couldn't share a bed. I slept with Amie, Paul slept with Ryan. That was the start of our marriage, and we still laugh about that night.

The transition from college student to instant mother, and wife soon thereafter, was a really difficult one for me. I'm the only child of a completely nontraditional set of parents. I love my parents deeply, but I can't say that they really showed a lot in terms of modeling for marriage and somewhat traditional parenting. My mom didn't cook a lot or worry about housekeeping as much as some people; she was a career educator and worked pretty constantly. My dad was a minister, and the more stay-at-home parent. He was also an alcoholic (he's now been sober for decades) and severely bipolar. So, living with and marrying a man who had come from a normal and traditional upbringing was a definite change.

I went into my new roles with near-obsessive attention to detail. In my mind, I was going to have the cleanest house, make the best meals, be at every school event looking fabulous, create culinary masterpieces for their school lunches, paint murals on their bedroom walls of their favorite things, knit them beautiful hats and mittens, and be the perfect partner for Paul. And I was going to do that all while working full-time. Heck, I was even going to throw in going to graduate school for an advanced degree in psychology at the same time.

Yeah, *right*. As if it were all going to be that easy.

It was a struggle, not put on me by Paul, but completely self-inflicted with a little help from Amie who wanted to make sure that I understood how their biological mom would have done things. To this day, the words "potato logs" push my emotional buttons, as for a long time, every time I made a meal with potatoes, Amie would tell me, "Mom would make potato logs with this."

Thankfully, Paul was patient and supportive beyond belief, and then I found the most amazing therapist who helped me start to let go of my control issues and helped us figure out how to make our new family work.

In the midst of trying to figure all of that out, Samuel Michael Francoeur was born in July of 1993 after a hellish pregnancy. Working as a paraeducator with a special needs student, I'd been kicked in the stomach when I was just about six months along, putting me on bed rest for months. When I went into labor, my doctor was away, and the "sub" didn't know Sam was caught in the umbilical cord. More than a day after I'd gone into full labor, he was born dark blue with an Apgar of zero, and was rushed from the delivery room. Sam's first couple of days were rough: he couldn't keep sugar in his bloodstream; they were feeding him by a tube down his nose; he couldn't figure out how to nurse (or maybe I couldn't figure it out); and he had a pointy head from the forceps that had been used to extricate him during delivery. He had long black hair, and once his head started returning to a reasonable shape, his hair stuck straight up in a funny, fuzzy halo.

The first thing anyone noticed about Sam, even at a few days old, was that he didn't sleep; he was almost eerily aware of everything. With his death, I began to wonder if somehow his soul had always known his time would be short, so he didn't waste too much of it by sleeping. As a tiny baby, Sam watched other people constantly, paying attention to them with an odd focus. One of the first pictures we have of him once he came home from the hospital is of Ryan reading *Green Eggs and Ham* to him, and Sam, only a few days old, was looking at Ryan intensely. Late at night, after the older kids were in bed, we'd sit on the couch and watch a little TV, and Sam would lie between us and just watch us.

Within a really short time period, Sam started talking. He could talk in full sentences long before he could walk. And he would start a conversation with every person he met—I mean, *every single person*. He talked to the store clerks, the mailman, anyone on the street. When he was a toddler, I'd walk down the street with him and all these adults would say, "Hi, Sam!" because they knew him, and he knew them. Everywhere we went with Sam, we had to keep an eye on him because he'd wander off to have a conversation or, joy of joys, meet someone new.

But with that joy and enthusiasm came another side. Sam also could be incredibly stubborn. When he got mad as a toddler, he'd hold his breath until he turned blue. I'm not exaggerating. He'd turn a dark blue standing in the corner because he was so sure it was an affront to have to stand in time-out. After all, he was always certain that he'd been right in the first place, and we were just silly adults telling him he was wrong. After having had so many time-outs in the corner, he told us he was going to build a *round* house when he got older so there wouldn't be any corners. The funny thing was, though, that even when he got mad and was in trouble, as soon as the time-out was over, the sunshine that was Sam would come back, and he never held a grudge.

From the moment he was born, there was nothing that Sam wouldn't do for Amie and Ryan; they were his heroes. He followed them like a little puppy and was often encouraged to do silly things for their amusement, such as dancing the Macarena over and over or repeating "Hey Diddle Diddle." When they would go see their biological mom, Sam was so lonely. He couldn't wait for them to come back.

In July of 1997, Paul and I finally went on a honeymoon to Spain. Leaving little Sam for that long was a struggle, but we wanted (after our fifth anniversary) to finally have a special vacation, just the two of us. Sam stayed with my parents, Ryan went to see his biological mom, and Amie went to Georgia with her Memere.

In the months leading up to the trip, we had told Sam all about the places we were going to see and gave him a notebook with maps of Spain and information about sites so he could follow along—that kid loved maps from the time he was tiny. As we planned, we told Sam, then four years old, that we were also going to Africa, specifically Morocco. He was so fascinated by that idea and kept asking Paul if he was going to see Tarzan in Africa.

On the way home from our trip, having landed in Boston, we stopped at a local grocery and got Sam a banana; Paul told him he'd gotten it wrestling with Tarzan. One of my favorite memories of Sam (and there are a lot of them) is of him up in a cherry tree when we drove down the driveway. He was waving away, happy to see us, and yelling to Paul, asking if he'd really met Tarzan. I never actually knew if he thought we'd brought that banana all the way from Africa or not.

In May of 1998, our Ben was born. All through my pregnancy, Sam had talked to the baby, calling him Bubba. He would stand next to me in the kitchen, and talk to my abdomen, telling Bubba everything about his day, what they were going to do together when Bubba was born, and every single time, Sam would say, "I love you, Bubba" at the end of the conversation. When Sam came to the hospital to meet Ben, he walked in and said, "Hi, Bubba," and Ben turned his head to look at Sam. Ben was barely two hours old, but he knew *that* voice, and it was one he wanted to be near. That was the moment when one of the greatest loves in the world became visible. Sam loved Ben with a devotion that was almost fanatical from the time he knew I was pregnant, and Ben felt the same way. Like Sam, Ben started talking very early. The funny thing was that he could say "rhinoceros" but he couldn't say "Sam." Instead, Ben would make this odd loud sound, like *Hrrmmm* for Sam, and Sam would immediately respond. Sam loved that Ben had a unique name for him.

When Ben was six, on his first day of first grade, he fell down the stairs, fracturing his skull. Sam was there when it happened and screamed for us to come help. Sam was the one who waited for the ambulance at the top of the driveway and guided the EMTs to his brother's side. The long days when Ben was in the hospital? Sam called, visited, wrote him notes, sat next to him in the hospital, perching on this huge chair because he couldn't lie down next to him because Ben couldn't be jostled, and brought him endless cups of ginger ale. When Ben finally came home from the hospital, Sam spent so many hours reading to him, keeping him company, and even gave up his own recess in grade school so he could check on Ben and walk him carefully around the playground when he couldn't join in the games yet. *That* was the level of their devotion to each other.

This was Sam. Sam was love—pure and simple. He loved the people in his life with clear, consistent, unwavering, unflinching, love—love filled with wonder, love with almost fanatical loyalty. He had the ability to love without judgment, without preconceived notions. Even in moments of great frustration and hurt later on in his life as he struggled, his love was still as deep and profound.

That is who Samuel Michael Francoeur has always been to me—love and light—and suddenly that light and love seemed to have been extinguished.

October 10, 2013 –
Friends, Soccer, and Cookies

So here we were. It was now October 10th, 2013. We had tried to get organized; we knew when and where the service would be, and we knew who was going to do what. Paul had changed his mind and wanted to speak too, so we worked on that together. Loved ones were beginning to arrive from out of state, and we were making sure that everything that needed to be done had been.

Ben had stayed home on October 9th, but on the morning of the 10th, he announced that he wanted to go to school that afternoon, just for a bit, and to play in the soccer game that afternoon. We were shocked, but had told him over and over that he needed to let us know what he needed, and we would make it happen. If he wanted to go to school and play soccer, we would make it so.

As we waited for Ben to get ready to go to Otter Valley, we sat and talked about how there was still so much to coordinate for the service. My dad would deliver the eulogy. Paul and my mom and I would speak, Sam's friend Kirsten wanted to say a few words, Linnea was writing something and sending it from Bhutan to be read, Amie was to read a poem (actually a song from the movie "Spirit"), Sam's friend Will was going to play the piano, and our friend Ashton would be in charge of the music on CD.

We decided that we wanted two of Sam's teachers to speak if they were willing to. Now, if you know Otter Valley Union High School, you know there are no two people seemingly more different than Jeff and Larry. Jeff is a theater teacher—amazing, creative, quiet, gentle, focused, and seems a bit shy. Larry is tall, big, loud, and scary as can be if you don't know him. These two men were such important parts of Sam's life at OV. With Jeff, it was love at first meeting. Sam would have jumped off a bridge if Jeff had told him to—in Sam's mind there was no director smarter or more talented. Larry? Well, that was another story. When Sam had found out he was going to have Larry for chemistry early on in high school, he called us as we were driving bumper-to-bumper on the Massachusetts Turnpike. Sam was in absolute hysterics, sobbing, begging us to get him out of having Larry as a teacher. But at OV, Larry is the only chemistry teacher, so Sam had to suck it up, and over time, one of his greatest friendships had formed. The day before he died, Sam went to OV to see if Larry was around. Sam loved the loud, bossy man with every ounce of his being, and Larry loved him just as much in return.

So on October 10th, we drove Ben to Otter Valley, and met with his and Sam's guidance counselor about Ben's return to classes as she wanted to make sure his needs were met in his own state of grief. After the meeting, we kissed him goodbye in the hallway, and we watched these amazing young men, Ben's friends, form a phalanx of protection around him in the hallway, being with him in the only way they knew, silently protecting him from others rushing to express their sorrow, keeping the crowds away unless he wished otherwise. They all were more dressed up than usual, partially for their upcoming game, but also out of their deep respect for the situation. Their faces as Ben joined them showed their love, their pain, and their fierce loyalty to him—all in silence through these long looks. There were all these strange adolescent chest-bump hugs, without words being spoken. Our cold terror at letting him out of our sight was replaced by some comfort that those boys would not let anyone or anything near him unless he was ready. As they started to move away in unison, all of these boys looked at Paul and me, their eyes glistening with tears as they nodded solemnly at us.

That was one of the things that I have learned over and over in this process. Often the younger generation, who doesn't have as much experience with loss and the proper protocols of grief, have led the way in compassion and love and dignity by just following their hearts. No one told these boys what to do that day; all they were told was that Ben was going to be there after the lunch break, and that he had a meeting in Guidance before going to class. They figured the rest out on their own.

Then we met with Larry and Jeff, and the most amazing, odd, unexpected thing happened. We thought Jeff (who never speaks in public) would hesitate about speaking, yet he agreed immediately. Then we asked Larry, who hesitated, not sure if he could do it, but he said he would somehow manage.

Then there was another odd conversation at Otter Valley that centered on Sam's spirit. It was the first time that someone told us that his spirit had clearly visited them, and had a message for us, but it would not be the last time someone told us that. Keep in mind that Sam had only been gone from this earth for a day, and already, his spirit had visited someone with a message for us. While we now have come to peace with people coming to us with "messages," then it was like we were in a parallel universe or something.

An hour later, we went out to the soccer field to see Ben play. Amie and Ryan were there, as well as Will, my parents, Paul's parents, and a bunch of Sam's friends—all had come to watch Ben.

Players who hadn't seen Ben earlier in the day hugged him. Members on the other team who had known Sam or his little brother came over to express their condolences to Ben. His team almost hovered over him in that game, although he played like a demon, maybe getting out some of his hurt. As we watched the game, parents and grandparents came over and hugged us, showing us they cared; teachers from the school came out to see us. They all knew Sam. *Everyone* knew Sam. People who we didn't know knew Sam—*knew* him. Ben's coach came up in the stands and cried with us. We cried. Lots of people cried.

After the game, we waited for Ben, the rest of the family and friends having packed up to meet us back at the house. As we stood by the car, so ready to get away from the crowd for a while, Ben came up through the bleachers with a box in his hand and a slightly bemused look on his face. When he reached us, he held out a box. "Garrett made me cookies."

How sweet, I thought. Ben continued. "He said he made a dozen, but he ate nine of them, so he left three: one for me, you, and Dad."

Somehow, the beauty in the love of Garrett making cookies, combined with him eating three-quarters of them, made us laugh. It was the first time we had really laughed in two days, and to this day, we still bring up "the cookie incident" and laugh.

CHAPTER FIVE

Planning and Saying Goodbye

Over the next days, we planned for the service; we organized, we grieved, and we tried to survive. Kids kept coming through the door, bringing meals from their parents, bringing meals they had made themselves, bringing pictures or pieces of music. My cousin Ed came from Indiana, providing much-needed love, support, humor, and logistical support. Ed had lost his brother when he was in high school, and we've been close our entire lives. He became the person who "made sure the trains ran on time" during that week. When Ben wanted to go see a friend for a bit (he didn't drive yet) and we couldn't get away, Ed drove him. When we didn't have anything planned for dinner, Ed got Chinese. When we forgot to eat or drink, Ed shoved cider in our hands to keep us going. All the while, he made us laugh by doing silly things—things we could laugh about. He spoke in various accents, made comments about the huge van he had rented at the airport, and regaled us with accounts of trying to take a shower in the tiny (and rotting) cottage he was renting while here.

In those days, we began to learn a truth that we have to remember even now—that we all grieve differently. Not better or worse, not less or more, just different. For me, right from the beginning, I needed to look at photos of Sam. I needed to see those beautiful, smiling images, his love shining out of every one. If I didn't look at the photos, my mind filled with the awful image of him dead on that floor. So I looked at pictures then, and I still do. Other members of the family can't look at the photos. Some can watch videos of Sam; others can't. That was one of the most important things I learned: to accept that not everyone does things the way I do, and that it doesn't mean their grief is any less than mine.

On that Saturday morning, Amie and I were supposed to be working on the photo displays. My friend Sally had brought us easels, and my friend Patty had gone on a printer ink run for us, so we were ready. Just then, three of Ben and Sam's friends showed up at the front door with a covered casserole dish in their hands—they had made us a breakfast casserole, thinking it would help. Knowing these boys well, we knew that this was such a huge gesture of love and devotion—their culinary prowess was typically limited to Hot Pockets or Buffalo chicken dip. So we welcomed them inside, and visited with them, so thankful for their love. Just as they left, Will's mom walked through the door with a casserole, and then Kirsten and her sister arrived. In some ways, none of this was abnormal—Sam had brought people into the house all the time. But in the midst of this chaos, Amie had a meltdown. Our beautiful, so pregnant, tired, grieving daughter had a meltdown as she sat there sobbing about the fact that we were supposed to be making the photo displays, and if we didn't get to them soon, they wouldn't be ready for the service.

That moment taught me so much about grief. Sam's big sister needed to show her love for him by making beautiful photo displays of his life—she wanted them to be perfect, and with all the noise and people coming and going, we weren't getting them done. With that, we took all the supplies, went to my bedroom, shut the door and stayed put, crying through our laughter and memories until those displays were done.

On that same day, as a family, we were able to write letters to Sam to be put in the wooden box with his ashes. We wrote notes, we added Legos, we added seeds—all symbols of our love for him, and things he loved.

That Saturday afternoon, we went to the meeting house to get it ready for Sam's service. Getting out of the car, my parents were already there, and an elderly woman was waiting for us; this was a woman who had helped us decorate the meeting house so many years before for our wedding. She had helped plan my bridal shower. She had helped throw the baby shower for me when I was pregnant with Sam. And without being asked, she was there again, showing the circle of life and love around us.

We decorated the room with the funny-looking squashes Sam had loved so much. We tucked heads of garlic and hot peppers on each window sill, then arranged the picture of him on a table at the front of the meeting house, knowing that his ashes would be placed there next to the picture. We brought Legos, his baby blue Crocs, the easels of the pictures of him. And, last but not least, we brought a pan of brownies with the center piece cut out, just like he had done so many times in his life.

As we finished decorating, that friend told us that she would be bringing cookies the next day, and knew that her daughter was too, because they'd seen my request online for refreshments. With hugs, we thanked her for her time, and left her sitting with my parents, praying with them.

———

On that Sunday, October 13th, we held a celebration of Sam's life at the Leicester Meeting House. I remember getting dressed for the service, unsure as to what to wear to bury our child—to bury the hopes and dreams we'd had for him. Should I wear black because my soul was so dark and sad, or should I wear bright colors because Sam was (and is) a rainbow to me, to us? I finally decided to wear something brighter, but just before we left the house, I had a meltdown because I hadn't shaved my legs. You may think, what the heck, who would care? *I* cared. I felt I was disrespecting Sam because my legs were hairy. I know… it makes no sense to anyone reading this unless you've lived through a moment like that, but just know that leg stubble was my personal undoing.

We arrived early to the service, in the huge white van that had been the only available rental vehicle when Ed arrived in Burlington. We drove down to the town center, a small green with the meeting house next to the school and parking lot, figuring that we would be so early that we could park right next to the brick building.

Not on your life.

The place was mobbed.

I mean, *mobbed.* People parked up and down the street, the lot was full, and people were parked on the lawn. Cars were even parked all the way down a side road. People were everywhere—tall, short, white, black, dread-locks, shaved heads, bare feet, wheelchairs, three-piece suits, top hats, cocktail dresses, high heels, ankle monitors from the corrections department, mud boots, manure boots. Old, young, pregnant, nursing, babies, high schoolers, it just went on and on. People we knew, and people we didn't. *So many people had come out of love to celebrate Sam's life. So, so many people.*

Again, how could this be happening?

I don't remember a lot of the service, just bits and pieces. Walking into the meeting house, an older usher from the funeral home approached me. "Mrs. Francoeur, I am so sorry."

Looking at him, he seemed vaguely familiar, but I couldn't place him. "Thank you."

"When I heard it was Ben's brother, it broke my heart. Ben's such a good boy."

I suddenly realized who he was. He was Ben's beloved middle school baseball coach. "Coach, thank you. Thank you for being here."

"You're welcome. Come, let's take you to your seat. I'll take care of Ben."

I remember that Linnea's words were supposed to be read by a relative of ours, but minutes before the service started, we found out he'd taken ill. What were we going to do? We could barely stand the thought of reading our own piece; we certainly couldn't read hers too. Ryan? No, he said he didn't want to say anything, and neither did Ben. Other relatives? No, they didn't want to either. Across the room, sitting in a sunbeam from the large windows, Garrett sat wiping his tears.

Paul whispered to me. "Garrett. Let's ask Garrett?"

I looked at him in confusion. "Garrett?"

"Yes. Or is that too much to ask?"

By this point, Will, sitting in his tux and top hat, his converse sneakers peeking out on the piano pedals, was playing soft music, music that I know now was a medley of Twiddle tunes. I nodded my head. "Garrett's comfortable in front of a crowd. If he doesn't feel comfortable, he'll say so."

No surprise, he agreed. Later, in his good suit, so painfully serious, he read Linnea's words which had come all the way from Bhutan:

No words can summarize a life like Sam's. Nothing and no one can capture the incredible personality of someone who lived with nei-

ther fear nor boundaries, albeit for better or worse. His practically flawless Arlo Guthrie impression and inability to successfully make Annie's Mac 'N' Cheese by himself are things we must hold onto in our hearts. A person is immortalized in the memories you choose to keep. This is the one I want to share with you.

One summer's morning, in 2011 I think, Kris and I were sitting at their kitchen table—probably drinking coffee—after Sam had been sent out to finish some chores in the backyard. Before too long, the strangest noises starting coming in through the back windows, and I went to look through the small attached porch. There was Sam; barefoot, in boxers and a t-shirt, with his hair a little too long per usual, chasing after one of the alpacas that he'd purposefully set loose with the intention of playing tag. His arms were flung up over his head, waving side to side and he was screaming with a noise only similar to that of Zoidberg from Futurama (Can anyone in the meeting hall make that noise for an example, since I'm not there to do it?) That poor alpaca was running in circles absolutely terrified, with Sam quickly closing in on its tail. When the animal finally gave up and stood still, Sam gave it this strange little head bump with the greatest sense of accomplishment before leading it back into the fence. When he looked up and realized that I'd been watching the entire time, we fell to pieces laughing for what felt like five minutes and when Kris quickly asked, "what's he doing out there?" I dutifully responded, "oh...just finishing his chores."

Sam showed me how to start a campfire with only an empty pack of cigarettes, three matches and a wet log. To this day, I have no idea how he did it. Sam taught me to jump into the darkness and always trust that he would be there waiting. His smile could melt the hardest of hearts, and his light brightened the darkest of rooms even when he feared it was going out. Sam's goal was never to be perfect; it was to be happy. When he loved something or someone, it was with a love that never wavered. Sam's craziness will be missed every day for the rest of eternity and every blue sky will forever be his.

I remember Ashton ran the music. I remember our friend Lyle, his son Zach who was a good friend of Sam's, and his daughter Taylor, who was Sam's first real girlfriend, sitting up front and looking at them, helped. Hannah nursed little Grace, which seemed to fit the moment. I remember how little Ben looked, how lost Ryan looked, how Amie tried to hold back her sobs as she read "I Will Always Return" by Bryan Adams, Paul's arms wrapped around her. Sam *so* loved the movie *Spirit*.

I hear the wind call your name

It calls me back home again

It sparks up the fire—a flame that still burns

Oh it's to you I'll always return

I still feel your breath on my skin

I hear your voice deep within

The sound of my lover—a feeling so strong

It's to you—I'll always belong

Now I know it's true

My every road leads to you

And in the hour of darkness darlin'

Your light gets me through

Wanna swim in your river—be warmed by your sun

Bathe in your waters—cos you are the one

I can't stand the distance—I can't dream alone

I can't wait to see you—yes I'm on my way home

Oh I hear the wind call your name

The sound that leads me home again

It sparks up the fire—a flame that still burns

Oh, it's to you—I will always return.

Then Paul and I stood together to give our eulogy.

When Sam died this week, we struggled with whether or not to have a public service, but we quickly realized that Sam should not go out on a whisper, but in a joyous celebration of who he was. We picked this spot, because here, on this same platform, Paul and I got married, and Amie and Ryan took vows with us to be a family. This is where our family officially began, and we come back today to celebrate Sam in our family spot.

Some of you knew Sam, some of you know US and heard us talk a lot about Sam.

Let's be realistic. Sam was not a saint, and he would guffaw at the thought of anyone saying he was. He could be loud, sloppy, opinionated to a fault, and sometimes a little smelly. He could NOT hang a towel to dry or shut a light off. He killed cell phones with amazing regularity, and lost some of his few possessions on a daily basis. Having said that, no one that knows Sam would ever deny that he is the kindest, most open-minded and accepting individual we have ever known. Sam never met an individual that he didn't love wholeheartedly. Sometimes he would come home talking about someone new he'd met, and we'd inwardly think "uh huh," but he'd talk about all the amazing things about that person. Sam led the family in teaching us all how to accept differences of opinion, differences of philosophies, of looks, and reminded us when we needed it that love is what matters.

Sam is equally enthusiastic about everything else. Every meal was the BEST meal ever. Every movie was the best one he'd ever seen. "Mom and Dad, you HAVE to read this book, it's the best one ever written." Don't we all wish we could roll through life with that kind of enthusiasm?

From the day Sam was born, he jumped into life with his whole heart. Sam could talk before he could walk. Anyone surprised by that? He didn't take naps as a baby; the world was too interesting to sleep. He jumped into his role as little brother with as much joy and love as Amie and Ryan did into being the older sister and brother. There was NOTHING he wouldn't do when asked by Amie or Ryan, hence the great Macarena video that some of you have seen. When Ben was born, Sam took on the role of being the big brother with just as much passion. No one who knows Sam didn't see his absolute love, devotion to and pride in his siblings, and in his whole family—and God help anyone who messed with those he loved.

Sam knew what he wanted in life. One of the things Sam taught us as parents was the acceptance that what WE wanted for him was not necessarily what he wanted. And when Sam wanted something, he usually went ahead and got it, like the fact that he didn't like the edge pieces on brownies, so if a fresh pan was left out in the kitchen, the next time we came into the kitchen, it would have a great big piece taken out of the center, and he would grin when I growled about it. Life was too short for edge pieces.

As parents, Sam was, well Sam. He gave us some of the greatest moments of joy, and equal proportions of heartburn. You could NOT win an argument with that kid! No matter what the situation, even really difficult ones, the conversation ended with all involved saying "I love you."

We will miss Sam more than we can say. Not having him call five times a day, starting the conversation with "what's up" is heart-breaking. We will miss the scraps of hair and mud in the bathroom, the ketchup caked on EVERYTHING, and his infectious smile as he shared something from his day with you.

We thank you for being here with us today, and for your support through this. More than anything, we thank you for your love of our Sam.

———

There are large black holes in my memory from that day. I remember my mother standing to speak—my tiny mother who normally looks so energetic and upbeat, looking so small and sad, but her words rang through the meeting hall as she used her best teacher voice. I remember is that she actually mentioned drugs in her words, about them taking Sam from us. I remember my father giving his eulogy and the prayers, him sitting at a small table at the front of the meeting hall, his hands shaking with emotion. But even in his own grief, his voice stayed strong and clear—he was going to bury this beloved child well, no matter how much of a toll it took on him personally.

I remember the music we played for the service. Will played Twiddle's "Hattie's Jam," we played the Kosher Gelatin CD (a song written and performed by Sam and his friends), played a lot of Arlo Guthrie and America, then played Arlo's version of "Amazing Grace." I remember that's when I cried. That's when it seemed to hit me that we were actually saying goodbye to Sam, and Arlo's voice had the depth and the pain that I was feeling.

Then (I don't know why, but I'm so glad I did) I asked the congregation to give Sam a round of applause. It wasn't something I'd planned to do. I had stood to invite people out for cookies and cider, but then I just felt the need to ask them to make some joyous noise in his honor. As I said then, Sam so loved to hear people clap for him. It turned into a standing ovation that went on and on, tears running down faces, but the thunder of applause echoed through the area.

That night, one of his friends posted on Sam's Facebook page.

Much deserved standing ovation today, friend.

After the service, we all left the meeting house, going out into the sunshine. Stepping outside, I realized that there was this sea of people outside, hundreds of people who had come to honor Sam, but the meeting house was too small to hold them all. They had stood outside for more than an hour, unable to hear the service. Maybe they could hear the music? A friend later told me that they could hear "Amazing Grace" and the applause at the end, and that they had joined in, singing and clapping outside.

I remember the clothes the kids wore; how hard they had worked to dress up in Sam's honor, these beautiful, sometimes scruffy kids who had been part of our lives for years. They had slept in our living room in their boxers, often seemed to get cleaned up in our pool, and wore the same hoodies day in and day out, but for this, they wore suits and dresses. Some of the young women teetered around, unaccustomed to high heels. A lot of the suits clearly were borrowed and ill-fitting, ties tied poorly, but what love they showed in their attention to their clothing on that day. You dress up to show respect and reverence, and boy, did they do that.

I remember being outside receiving people. Paul and I had become separated in the crowd, each with our own line of people coming at us. I remember some of those who were there, some I don't, and I remember being approached by faces I just couldn't place.

Then I recognized one woman as the mother of a boy who had died of an overdose years before coming toward me. She was still standing, right? That had to mean it wouldn't always hurt this badly. As I hugged her, I begged, "Tell me it gets better."

She took a step back, holding my hands tightly and allowed for a long pause before she looked me straight in the eyes. "No, it doesn't get better. It gets *different*."

That couldn't be the truth! No one could live like this. She had to be lying. "No! Tell me it gets better."

She shook her head, pulling me close to hug me again. "I can't, my friend. It doesn't get better, but you will learn to live with it. It gets *different*."

For a long time, I was *so* very angry at her for saying that. I had wanted her to tell me that the pain would subside, and she didn't. She told the truth, and now, looking back, I can say that was the kindest thing she could have done.

Partway through the line, a group of kids from UVM stepped forward. Now, UVM was something I felt so badly about. I felt that I had pressured Sam into going to college to make *me* happy. This group of amazing young people stepped forward, hugged me, told me how much they loved Sam, and I brokenly said I was sorry that I had forced him to go to college.

One of them, one of Sam's roommates, looked at me and took my hands. "Kris, we're so thankful you did! If he hadn't gone to UVM, we wouldn't have met him." To this day, that fills me with warmth. Even if I had pressured him, it still meant something to these amazing young people.

At one point, I felt someone behind me, and I turned to find my cousin Ed standing there. Without preamble, he shoved a glass into my hand. "Cider. Drink it before you collapse."

I took a sip, feeling the cold tartness dance across my tongue. "What about Paul?"

"I just gave him some too." He gestured behind him. "Do you want a cookie?"

I looked at the picnic tables on the lawn and saw that they were covered, tops and benches, with platters of cookies and brownies. More cookies than

I'd ever seen in my life. It turned out that all these people had responded to my request, and they'd brought treats that Sam had enjoyed with them. There were cookies *everywhere*, and it was such a visible sign of the love he had inspired.

———————

After receiving hundreds of people, we had to do what we all dreaded so much: we had to leave the group and go to the cemetery for the private committal service. We couldn't pretend any more that we didn't have to go to the cemetery. We couldn't pretend that this was just a community event.

That day was beautiful with the foliage near peak, the little cemetery a peaceful spot. Sam's plot was in the front row, and we made cracks about how much he'd always loved to be in the front row. We sat on padded folding chairs, the legs sinking into the earth, so I remember feeling that I was literally off-kilter. My father read the prayers of committal, and then it was time to go. Except I couldn't. I couldn't stand the thought of putting his remains into the ground. Logically, I knew he was gone, but I could still hold onto that box. Putting it in the earth meant that he was truly, irrevocably gone. I remember sitting cross-legged on the cold, damp ground in my black skirt and blue sweater with a rainbow scarf, smelling the leaves, holding that small wooden box in my arms, unable to breathe, my heart aching more than I can explain. Paul wrapped his arms around me as we sobbed, unable to speak. Ben leaned in while Amie and Ryan knelt next to me, all of us clutching each other. It truly was a circle of equal love and pain, as we just held each other and sobbed. *How could Sam be reduced to this little box of remains? How could we say goodbye? Would anything ever be right again?*

That night, we ate as an extended family, barely talking, exhausted and broken, and went home. It wasn't until much later that we would find out about the trip Sam's friends took that night in his honor.

CHAPTER SIX

Our New Lives and Garlic

The next morning, Ben went to school, Ryan left to go back to New Hampshire, and we tried to figure out what to do next. So many logistics to still take care of for Sam, so many stupid details. Where to start? Did we start with dealing with the things like his lease and clothes and stuff at the farm, or did we clean up our house which had been ignored for days even as all these people had walked through?

Gathering my thoughts, I looked out the window and noticed the strangest rainbow splayed across the sky on what was a crystal clear sunny day. Viewing it from our deck, it was clearly coming from the cemetery area, and it was an up-down rainbow, not the normal arc. That was my first post of thankfulness on Facebook.

Monday, October 14, 2013

In the midst of great sadness can come a moment of great beauty—
this morning there was a beautiful rainbow over Leicester.

Over the next couple of days, I don't remember much except for a few truly memorable phone calls. (Keep in mind that "memorable" doesn't necessarily always mean good.) In speaking to Sam's landlord, asking if we could establish a payment plan on his owed rent, she expressed how much she loved Sam, and told us to forget his debt. That was a beautiful call that filled my heart, reminding me of the goodness in people. Then I made calls on his student loans and after having to tell person after person that my son was dead, one awful person simply stated that they could only talk to the account holder. I was shuffled from one person to the next, put on hold more times than I could count, transferred over and over with no one willing to resolve anything or guide me. I made my way through to the final supervisor who again, told me that they couldn't close the account until they spoke to Sam. I admit it—*I lost it.* I remember screaming, "He's dead! I'd love to be able to talk to him, or have him talk to you, but I can't." She then told me I would need to talk to *her* supervisor… I wish I were making this up.

Paul and I had to figure out what to do with ourselves while Ben was at school each day, since I had been given some time off. Actually, incredibly, I was told to take all the time I needed; the support was unparalleled. We decided that we were just going to stay home for a week and a half following his death, but after the service and all the details, we ended up rambling around the house. That's where the garlic really comes into this story.

For the last six months of his life, Sam had worked at Good Earth/Neshobe Farm in Brandon, Vermont. He'd worked as an intern for our friend Hannah, who also happens to be our former daughter-in-law (she had been married to our daughter Amie.) Sam found his vocational calling on that farm. Farming, specifically vegetable farming, brought him joy in a way that nothing else did. Digging in the dirt day in and day out made him happy, just plain happy, and gave him a sense of peace that was visible to anyone who knew him. Sam could, and would, talk about *anything*—but when he started farming, he'd come home and talk for hours about what he'd planted and what he'd learned that day, and how we could improve on our own farming. At a time when there had been a fair amount of strife between all of us over his substance abuse and legal issues, talking about farming was a welcome reprieve.

For Mother's Day 2013, Sam brought me two hot pepper plants that he'd helped grow at the farm, knowing how much I like making my own hot sauce. We make our own hot sauce, can all sorts of things, ferment kimchi and sauerkraut, things like that. Giving me pepper plants was both useful and incredibly thoughtful. Shortly before his death, Sam brought home some garlic he'd helped to grow, so proud of it, so enchanted by it. The idea is that you take one clove of garlic, plant it properly in the fall, and leave it until the next year, and if you did the simple steps of mulching, weeding, cutting the scapes and then harvesting it, from each clove you would have a full head of garlic—to Sam, that was miraculous.

For his service, we'd decorated the meeting house with garlic, hot pepper plants, squashes, all things he'd helped to grow. No gladioli, no roses, just produce. Now, as we tried to figure out how to keep going, how to keep busy so that the crushing pain wouldn't destroy us, we decided to plant his garlic in a box on the lawn to help keep his spirit alive. He loved the garlic and we loved him, so growing his garlic would be a way to keep that love alive. It made perfect sense to us, even if not to anyone else.

So we googled how to grow garlic, Paul built a box, and we planted it. Now if you haven't planted garlic before, Sam was right, it *is* miraculous. You fill a box with well-fertilized, rich soil mixed with sand so it's light enough for the cloves to grow. Each clove is nestled about two inches deep and six inches apart, with the root end pointing down into the earth. Once they are all planted, you pat the soil over them, cover it all with 8-9 inches of mulch, and wait for the magic to come the next year.

As we planted each clove, Paul and I talked about Sam. In hindsight, other than the first day, we had constantly been surrounded by people for days and days. This was our first time to talk alone, as the only two people in the world who each completely understood how the other felt. We cried; we laughed and made comments about how fitting it was to plant something smelly in a box of manure in his memory. Sam had touched each of those cloves, they were something he'd cared for, and we were now going to protect that legacy. When we were done, we sat in the sunshine and begged the universe to have let us do it correctly, so the garlic would grow in his honor. Over the next months, we visited those boxes a lot, talking to the garlic, willing it to flourish. Who am I kidding? Almost five years later, we still visit the garlic boxes and talk to Sam and his garlic, keeping it going with ferocious loyalty.

About a week after Sam died, we began to get his belongings back. His friend Arlie, who also lived at the farm, washed everything he could find and brought it home to us. We went to the farm to look for everything else and it wasn't long before we realized that some "special" things were missing. I'm not saying anyone took anything; it was more likely that Sam was so disorganized that stuff got lost, but there was a core list of things we set out to find. Our friend Linnea posted online, hoping to help us.

My dear Facebook friends of Sam:

Kris (Sam's mom) sent me a message asking me to post this to you. Sam had a tendency to leave his belongings anywhere and everywhere, and the Francoeur family is on the lookout for a few things in particular. Her message is below.

"I am wanting people to be on the lookout for several things, and if they find them to return them to us—we are looking for his hemp necklace with the tree of life pendant, his (Kris's) iPod Touch, his Green Mountain Spinning Wheels long-sleeve t-shirt and hoodie, his Farmy t-shirt, his reggae lion shirt, his Arrested Development shirt, his kitten/shark shirt, any of his tie-dyes, and his flannels (other than those we have already given away). Thank you, thank you!"

Take a look around and see if you can find any of these things, they would love to have them back.

Much love <3

The list of things we would have liked to get back was pretty long, but Sam had been pretty disorganized about a lot of his belongings over time, so we had no idea where anything might be. The list we settled on was: my iPod (which he had filled with his choice of music for me), his shirts from our spinning wheel business that he wore all the time because he was so proud of us, a couple of his t-shirts that made him laugh, his tie-dyes because that boy loved anything tie-dyed, and his flannels because, frankly, we all wanted to curl up in them, to feel his presence and smell his unique scent.

The Farmy shirt and the hemp necklace were two items that were even more important to him, and therefore to us. When he found his calling on the farm, we'd seen a Farmy (not Army) shirt online and had gotten it for him for his 20th birthday, and he absolutely loved it. Paul wanted that back so he could wear it in Sam's honor, and in honor of Sam's excitement about our own farm. The tree of life necklace was Sam's favorite necklace of all time, made by Linnea. He wore it faithfully until it fell off one day in his camper at the farm. We all knew how much it meant to him, and it was something that I wanted to be able to wear. Sam had told us that he was getting a tattoo of that particular tree on his 21st birthday.

Over the next weeks, Sam's things appeared on our porch. Not one, but two "Keep Vermont Weird" shirts came home, even though we had forgotten to list that shirt in the request. The Farmy shirt came home. Flannels, Crocs, and hats all came home. Sadly, his favorite necklace and iPod never made their way back. Somewhere out in the universe, I hope they are bringing their keepers joy.

CHAPTER SEVEN

The Boston Red Sox and a Gravestone

Over the next few weeks, we returned to work, we went to soccer games, we did laundry, and we tried to get through each day. We tried to figure out what to do with Sam's stuff, when just looking at his things could send us to our knees in grief. For example, his godawful orange baseball cap with the mesh backing? He'd won it at the local fair, and the thing is hideous. But when we found it in the trunk of the car where we had put his clothes from my parents' house, I looked at that stupid hat—one that I had hated so much and thought made him look stupid—and I ended up sitting in the driveway on the gravel, sobbing. It still smelled like him, and knowing that he would never wear it again was almost more than I could bear.

We paid the enormous bills for Sam's burial and service, thankful that we had a rider on our own life insurance policies, because no matter how frugal we had tried to be, without that insurance, the financial toll would have been significant. We closed bank accounts, we canceled the retirement fund Sam had been so proud to establish, and we tried to keep breathing.

One of the things that kept us going in those first few weeks were the Boston Red Sox. Now, if you know us personally, you know how much we love the Sox. But if you are getting to know us through this book, then you probably don't understand how important they are to us. Truck Day, when the Sox's equipment heads to Spring Training, is how I mark the days and know for certain that spring is coming. Opening Day at Fenway would be a national holiday in my world. Paul, Ben, Sam and I had gone to Red Sox games in Boston, Cleveland, and Toronto, and watched them on TV religiously.

In those first weeks, night after night, the three of us turned on the Sox. By the time the dinner dishes were done, we were *fried*. Beyond words, incapable of interacting, sick of trying to sound normal, whatever normal now was, we couldn't talk anymore. We were so tired, so sad, still so shocked, that by the end of a day of coping, the best we could do was sit together and watch the Sox. We couldn't talk about feelings anymore, we couldn't talk about how much every night that Sam didn't call made our hearts ache. All we could do was sit and yell for the Sox. That fall they won the World Series, and in my heart, I'm sure that Sam helped the Sox win, knowing that in particular Ben needed that moment of pure joy. That night was the first time since October 9th that I remember seeing a truly genuine and relaxed smile on Ben's face.

Here we were at the end of the second week since his death, and now we also had the chore of picking a gravestone for him. Helping your child pick a stone for an engagement ring is a joy; picking a stone to indicate your beloved child's bodily remains, not so much. Back to the funeral home we went, looking at all different types of stones, colors, styles, fonts, and quotes. We held back tears as we recalled taking Sam and Ben to the Barre Granite Museum—a fun trip, as so many countless others were.

We finally settled on a rough-cut stone, not polished, with his name, birth and death years, 1993-2013, and then a quote. Paul and I spent hours searching for the perfect quote about Sam. We looked at lyrics from his favorite songs, read quotes by his favorite writers, and thought about lines from movies he'd quoted over and over, and none of them fit.

Hours turned into days, and then Paul found the perfect one while googling quotes about love.

Thursday, October 17, 2013

"The greatest gift that you can give to others is the gift of unconditional love and acceptance."

It was, *is,* the perfect quote for Sam. No matter how hard Sam was struggling in his own way, his love of everyone was central to his being. He loved and accepted anyone and everyone. With shaking hands, we sent the quote to the funeral director so he could order the stone.

CHAPTER EIGHT

The Firsts

Another week passed, and we came to the first of the firsts. The first major family event after Sam's death was my birthday in late October. I was clear: I didn't want to celebrate the day, not then, not *ever*. How could I celebrate something as selfish as my own birthday when Sam was gone? How could I have cake and a special dinner when at least once a day I found myself sobbing uncontrollably, rocking, and struggling to breathe? All I wanted for my birthday was for Sam to come through the front door as he had so many times, slamming it as he shouted hello and then asked what was for dinner. All I wanted for my birthday was to hold him in my arms one more time. How could I celebrate my birthday feeling that way? Paul got it, and said that if that was what I wanted, he completely understood. My parents and in-laws? Not so much. In hindsight, I think they wanted to show me love and support, and in their minds, a birthday event was just the thing.

My birthday morning dawned—a Saturday. I had decided to get a pedicure, something I rarely do but absolutely love. I went to Middlebury, where I soaked my feet and watched the Middlebury Falls through the window. And I cried, and cried, and cried. Then, as the poor nail artist tried to figure out how to deal with me, she asked what color I wanted on my toes. Pink, I wanted pink, but then I told her that I wanted my left pinky toe nail to be painted bright green, as in my mind that signified that spring was coming, and

I needed to hold on until spring when I could again work the earth, and find the peace that gardening brings me.

I came home and cried again when I was handed a wrapped gift. I ran from the room, sobbing as I railed to poor Paul about how anyone could wrap a gift to me. How? I was so deep in my own grief, I couldn't see that my family wanted to show their love in the only way they knew.

In the end, it was an okay afternoon. Tears streamed down my cheeks the whole time, but we made it through it as well as any of us could. That night, I sat and read the notes of love and support my friends had posted on Facebook, especially those from Sam's friends who wanted to let me know that they loved us all. It helped—a little bit.

The next day I wrote:

Sunday, October 27, 2013

To all of my FB friends and family, thank you so much for the beautiful and loving birthday wishes, and for your amazing love and support in general. I (we) can't adequately express how much we appreciate your support and love, and how lucky we feel, even in the midst of our grief, to have you all in our lives.

Life rolled on. Halloween came and went. I know we carved some pumpkins, and fifteen-year-old Ben went trick-or-treating with friends, but I don't remember much else about it. It's funny. I do remember a family member making a snarky comment about him being too old to go trick-or-treating, but we felt that if he could have fun with his friends for a bit, that was great—certainly *we* weren't a lot of fun to be around right then.

Then November came. If you haven't lived it, you can't fully understand the searing pain when you pass milestones. November 1st of 2013 signified the first calendar month that Sam was not alive in, and I know that sounds strange, but it broke my heart anew. We were now living in a month that Sam would never see.

Each day, we took walks, we tried to eat carefully, made a point of staying hydrated, and tried to take time to pay conscious attention to our other children. When my cousin Ed left in October to go back to Indiana, he had pulled me aside and told me that if our other children lost us like he'd lost his mom for a while after his brother's death, he was going to come back and kick us. I held that thought in my head and heart—not the threat, but the need to remember our other kids in our fog of grief. I probably overcompensated, hovering over Ben in particular, calling Amie and Ryan obsessively, trying to remind them how much they are loved. Then I started seeing posts on Facebook about posting daily in November about things and people for whom you were thankful. So I started.

Saturday, November 2, 2013

In joining my friends who are posting daily about what they are thankful for, for yesterday (and every day) I am so thankful for my husband—I always knew how blessed I was in my marriage, but never realized it as clearly as lately.

Wow, truer words had never been written. Well-meaning jerks love to tell you that after the death of a child the majority of marriages fail, unable to endure such a tragedy (which isn't true statistically), and it's usually followed with a hug, and a comment like, "Just thought you should know." We talked about it as people said this to us and recognized that while we had faced many struggles over the years, we'd made it through, and we could do this too, together. We also talked a lot about how often Sam talked about how in love we are, and how proud he was of our family.

Just over two weeks after Sam's death, Paul and I had a "date." Anyone who knows us or knows our children knows that we have a date dinner each week. It started decades ago when we first got together and we were too poor to afford the luxury of a babysitter for Amie and Ryan. During those leaner times, we made frozen pizza for the kids and got them a video, and they had their own little party once a week while Paul and I set the table with special dishes we bought at the local TJ Maxx just for those nights, lit candles, and had a "fancy dinner." Back then, it was nothing fancier or better than our normal meals—we just tried to make it seem more like something special.

Over the years, the dinners have gotten better, but the concept endures. We make a dinner together, set the table nicely, light a candle or two, have a glass of wine, and focus on each other. The joke in the family and among friends is that unless it's an emergency, don't interrupt a date dinner. Seriously, even now, after more than twenty-six years of marriage, our children or their friends will call or message on Saturday night, then immediately send a text saying, "Sorry, forgot it's date night, I'll call you tomorrow."

So, here we were. Sam had been buried two weeks before, and somehow, we needed to remember why we were together as a couple. We grilled a good steak, made risotto, and had a glass of red wine. We sat at our table—our beautiful dining table that Sam had helped carry down our driveway one winter night with Paul when it had been delivered, and we toasted Sam. And we cried. Then we sat in front of the blazing fireplace and we cried some more. Somehow, finding comfort in the familiarity of a date dinner allowed us to open up about how much it all hurt. That night, as on every other night, I was so thankful that I have Paul as my partner on this journey.

———

Saturday, November 2, 2013

Today I am thankful for small acts of kindness, whether from humans or animals. Yesterday late afternoon I was really struggling, and as I was bringing the chickens in, one wasn't going in the coop. I was so mad and frustrated, and admittedly, I was kind-of yelling at the chicken, until I realized it was Fluffy, and she wasn't going in the coop because she was waiting for me to pet her. When I realized it, I sat down on the ground and held her, so thankful that she in some way realized I needed some company at that moment.

———

Fluffy... how I miss that chicken. She was one of our laying hens, but really, I think she was more of a dog or cat in a chicken body. She wanted to be held or carried, loved to visit with humans, and had a very strong and loyal personality. That day, she helped me more than I could tell her.

———

Sunday, November 3, 2013

Today I am thankful for the amazing young people who are the friends of our children—and along the way have become part of the family. Their support, humor, patience, and love are absolutely amazing!

———

This became a recurring theme in my posts, and in our lives. All of our kids have fabulous friends, and we've been close to them all. In the past couple weeks, we'd seen a new side to these young people, especially Sam's friends. We always knew that Sam had amazing friends. We'd watched them grow up, they'd stayed at our house more times than we could count, eaten us out of house and home, traveled with us, and essentially been part of the family. Now they showed up, and have steadily continued to check on us, check on Ben, just showing us the love they felt for Sam.

CHAPTER NINE

Worrying, Grieving, Knitting

In the midst of the pain and grief, we were now in November and we suddenly had health issues to deal with. Just before Sam's death, I had been diagnosed with diverticulitis, but then I also went in for a check-up, and due to something the doctor noticed, I was sent for an unexpected specialized mammogram. Keep in mind, this was just over three weeks after Sam's death, and now we were waiting for an appointment for *this*. We reached a point of gallows humor where we discussed that we weren't sleeping anyway, so staying up all night worrying wasn't going to rob us of much rest. We didn't dare tell our parents or our children, knowing they were already reeling, and then we had to agonize through a weekend until the appointment. Finally, on that Monday afternoon I wrote:

Monday, November 4, 2013

Today I am thankful for small breaks in sadness—and in particular, we took a walk today through the Middlebury College campus, and I found myself telling Paul all about happy memories—especially some silly ones from my freshman year. Thanks to Kristen, Heidi, Mary, Sagri, Jim, Steve, Harry, Jamida, Daanish and many others for those great memories.

I wrote this after the appointment where they said there was nothing wrong in the mammogram, and we could breathe again. We drove over to Middle-bury College, got lunch in the Grille, and walked around the campus. In the relief of the news (or lack thereof), we could actually find some enjoyment. It was such a relief to walk in the cold fall air, holding hands, talking about my pumpkin-carving parties when I was in college, and for almost an hour, we didn't talk about death or loss.

Tuesday, November 5, 2013

Today I am thankful for my children, all four of them. They have taught me about unending, deeper-than-I-can-express love—they make me proud, help keep me grounded, and give me hope even when hope is in small measure.

and

I am also so thankful for friends who are there when the meltdowns come, and who hand me the Kleenex, and just keep me company. For Amy and Patty and Laura—I am so thankful for your constant support.

My employer and co-workers were absolutely the best during this time. They gave me flexibility and support and loved us. In the midst of it all, three people in particular, my office companions, kept me safe and sane. They cried with me, kept me fed, reminded me to breathe, protected me when needed, barricaded my door when I was at my breaking point, and laughed with me when we could.

Wednesday, November 6, 2013

Today I am thankful for living in a place with such natural beauty that it sometimes takes my breath away.

Sam so loved the outdoors that I found myself spending more and more time outside, even as the weather got colder. Whether it was walking after work or sitting on the deck as the stars came out, when I was outside, I felt closer to his spirit.

Thursday, November 7, 2013

Today, I am thankful for technology—cell phones, internet, and FB, in particular. While I sometimes think badly of them, I am so thankful for having them right now, so that I can call someone (using Bluetooth of course) while driving home when I need a friendly voice, so I can be in touch with friends whenever the urge hits, and so I can hear from friends across the globe.

Friday, November 8, 2013

Today we are thankful for the friends with perfect timing on text messages or FB messages—their reaching out helps keep us going!

Saturday, November 9, 2013

Today I am thankful, again and still, for our wonderful friends who are there for us always. And in particular, I am thankful today for Linnea who helped us through a rough patch today by sharing an awesome video and by just being herself, and for Bamby who just is an amazing friend. Thank you!

Monday, November 11, 2013

Yesterday was a very hard day for us, and one in which I struggled mightily to remember what I was thankful for—and finally it hit me like a freight train, that the reason I was grieving so hard was because of how much I (we) love Sam—and in the morning light today, I can say that in looking back at yesterday, I am thankful for the depth of that love.

Thursday, November 14, 2013

I have not posted this week about being thankful, but I am still thankful for so many things: Monday—for being financially secure enough that even in the midst of this, we don't have to worry about bills as much as so many people do. Tuesday—for being able to get great pizza at Brandon House of Pizza—so glad they came back

after the flood. Wednesday—for friends who appear with meals or
treats, and have made the perfect ones. Thursday—for knitting and
spinning, for they help quiet my mind for a bit. Throughout it all, I
am also so very thankful for family and friends—how truly blessed
we are to have you in our lives.

———

Knitting… Thank God for knitting. I learned to knit as a child, at less than five years old, from my grandmother. I knit all the time—I mean, *all* the time. I knit in meetings, riding in any sort of transportation, watching TV, at my kids' games, the beach, anywhere. I always have a knitting project with me. I also spin fiber from our alpacas to make my own yarn, and knit with that. But now, in this haze of grief, I knitted around the clock. It was one of the few things that could quiet my brain in its relentless mantra of grief for even a few minutes. I became somewhat obsessed with knitting a particular cowl scarf for the women who were supporting me through this all (I used a pattern that I had designed myself that can be found in the last chapter). I call the pattern my "I love you" scarf, because as I knitted each one, I would tell Sam I loved him over and over. The pattern is a 3-stitch repeat, and it just worked as a way for me to express my love to him.

Eventually, I started being able to think of the recipients as I knit each of those scarves. A local yarn shop was going out of business around then, and I went and bought a ton of thick, soft yarn, picking colors for specific women. Then I would sit and knit and think about how much I loved each one of them. Some of them were my protectors and support at work: the friend who brought "random acts of baked goods"; the friend who regularly left flowers or a can of SPAM on Sam's grave; the mom who knit the most beautiful story prayer shawl for us; and so many other incredible women in my life. I knitted, thinking of Sam, and thinking of them, and really, knit all my love into those scarves. When each one was done, I wrote a note to the recipient about how much I loved them, wrapped them up, and put them in the mail. I wasn't at a point where I could hand them over in person, but I still wanted to show them my love.

Years later, it makes me smile how often I see those women around town with their scarves. Their love of me, of us, was such a gift, and my being able to give them something in return mattered more to me than probably to them.

CHAPTER TEN

Mental Health Service and the Stigma

Now we were firmly into November; we had survived the first month without Sam, and (finally) we were beginning to feel things other than just the crushing pain of the loss. I kept waiting, and continued to wait, for the "normal" stages of grief to occur, and what I have come to believe is that when you are talking about the death of a child, there is no "normal" to the process. In talking with other parents, I've heard of people covering the spectrum: everything from being incredibly angry, and so depressed they sleep constantly, to being overly energetic and sleep deprived, and everything in between. Other than my own guilt that I hadn't had Sam come home that night, most of the other emotions, like anger, had stayed at bay.

As we got further into November, I started to wrestle with other parts of Sam's story, and had to face the reality of how our local community, no matter how supportive and loving they were, viewed his cause of death.

Sam was sunshine, joy, and love. Sam also was deep lows when he was cycling down with his bipolar disorder. We'd taken him to be evaluated for depression after he'd left UVM in the spring of 2012, and he was diagnosed as being depressed. While he took medication for a while, that didn't seem to do anything except make him angry—something we weren't used to. In the midst of this, Sam had a great job working for the local mental health agency, working with adults with developmental disabilities, and he loved his clients.

71

He'd moved into an apartment with a friend, and we thought everything was going along pretty well.

What we didn't know was that he'd stopped taking his antidepressants, thinking they were bringing him down more than up, and he was using drugs and alcohol to self-medicate, to control his mood swings or numb himself at the very least. In recognizing our own failures, we didn't realize how badly he was slipping, as his apartment was about 45 minutes away, and we rarely went there. Sam came over almost every day, and when he was home, he seemed to be doing pretty well.

Then he got arrested for DUI in Middlebury and was also charged with having unprescribed Adderall with him—as he told me later, it was to calm him down. He lost his job due to the arrest, so he suddenly had no income and was feeling like a failure, knowing how disappointed we were with the situation and the huge legal bills—just fun all around. Add to it the fact that any sort of arrest in Addison County was announced in *The Addison Independent*, so *everyone* knew of his troubles.

Fast forward a couple months: we were still thinking he was suffering from depression and there was still no real progress. Paul and I went away to Lake Placid for a weekend, needing a break—it had been a tough winter with all of this. As we were driving home, Sam called and I put him on speakerphone. "Mom, Dad, I know what my problem is… I've got it!"

What the heck was he talking about? "What?"

"I'm bipolar! That's what it is. I'm not depressed; I'm bipolar. That's why the medication didn't work!"

Paul broke in. "Okay, buddy, how are you self-diagnosing this?"

"Dr. Earle gave me a book. I've been reading it, and I meet all the descriptions of being bipolar."

The conversation continued as long as we had cell service as we drove through the Adirondacks. Finally, as the call was beginning to break up, I promised him that as soon as we got to a place with real service, I would call Dr. Earle to set up an appointment to look at the possibility of bipolar disorder, which I did. As I made the call to the doctor, it hit me that this made perfect sense, and I felt so stupid for not recognizing it as a possibility. My dad is bipolar, I knew of the genetic component, yet I had never considered the possibility.

Later that week, Dr. Earle, an amazing doctor and human being, met with Sam, and told him he thought he was right, but that he didn't feel he was qualified to make the diagnosis, let alone prescribe medication for this, so we needed to find a psychiatrist.

This thrust us into a hellish nightmare of red tape. Considering what I do professionally, I was confident in my ability to deal with bureaucracies, yet I still found it almost impossible to get the system to work. Sam had a great private therapist but refused to go to the local mental health agency for therapy because he'd worked there, and he found it embarrassing. I totally understood why he didn't want to go there for treatment. The only local psychiatrist who took our insurance worked at that agency. Sam couldn't see the psychiatrist unless he was in therapy there. *Are you kidding me?* We had great insurance, the kid wanted—no, was *begging* for help, and they kept giving me the "rules" speech. Finally, in one of my better moments, I told the intake person to put me through to the supervisor, who eventually put me through to the head of the agency, and that conversation ended with me telling him that I would take it all the way to the governor to show how this agency was denying help to people in need (which I did, but that's a whole other story).

We tried the University of Vermont medical center, and they had a six-to-nine-month waiting list on adolescent psychiatric appointments. How, as a supposedly enlightened society, can we allow children to go months waiting for help? How? In desperation, I called an old friend who was a therapist in New Hampshire and begged her for help. She moved mountains and got us an appointment with the most amazing psychiatrist. He was out of state and not in the insurance network, and it cost us a small fortune, but it was so worth it.

———

One warm June 2013 morning, Ben, Sam, and I got in the car and drove to New Hampshire for the intake with the psychiatrist. Hours and hours later, Sam had a tentative diagnosis, an appointment for a full physical and blood tests, follow-up visits planned, and he had hope for the first time in a long while. After the appointment, we went shopping, and again, in what we refer to as a "Sam Moment," he met a clerk in the shoe store who commented on liking his Boondock Saints shirt, and before I knew it, Sam was helping her stock the shelves, and he'd made a new friend. When we left the store, this older woman gave Sam a hug. Yup, that was Sam. He made an immediate connection with a stranger, and what a beautiful thing that was to watch.

The three of us went out to lunch for fish and chips. Sam and Ben were on a roll that afternoon; they had me laughing so much my sides hurt. It was a perfect afternoon. We had hope and we had a plan.

Later that afternoon, as we drove home, Ben fell asleep as he usually does riding in a car. Quietly, I asked Sam about something he'd said in the appointment; that he'd known he'd had mood swings since he was about fourteen (he was nineteen now), and that he'd started smoking pot soon after because it helped him keep his moods in check. Trying not to cry, I asked him why he hadn't told us. He said that he knew we had so much on our plates with our older children, and with Ben's health issues. In the fall of 2012, Ben had a scare with a heart issue, and in the midst of all the tests, they found he had an incredibly rare infection caused by ticks (not Lyme) and was under pretty intense medical care for months. Sam said that because he was able to control it through pot, he hadn't wanted to worry us. I remember pulling off the road because I was crying so hard, and Sam hugging me much like you hug a young child. "Mom, let it go. You and Dad have done everything and more than anyone could do. It's okay. Let it go."

Years later, I still can't let it go. I am the child of a man with severe bipolar disorder, I have a Master's degree in Counseling Psychology, and I still couldn't see what was happening with my own precious child. Maybe if I had been able to see what was really happening, we could have gotten him the correct help earlier, and maybe, just maybe, he'd still be here with us.

Fast forward to November 2013, and I began to wrestle with those memories, wrestle with my own failure to protect him from himself. Through it all, I could at least feel like we'd been honest about how he died, and honest about his struggles. That was a conscious decision we made as a family—we said we would *never* hide from the truth.

We wouldn't hide. We would stand up straight and say that our beloved Sam had died of an accidental drug overdose. We would not pretend it was something else. We would let other families know it was okay to come out of the shadows.

That was how we felt until a dear friend was visiting with us and said, "You know, there was no reason that Ellie (my mom) should have said at the service that it was drugs. You should've just said it was a heart thing or said nothing at all about the cause. No one needed to know that it was drugs."

That was the moment when the reality of how his death was perceived became real.

CHAPTER ELEVEN

The Tree, Theater, Deliberate Gratitude, and the Dreaded Thanksgiving

It was November 2013, and here I was struggling with my grief and regrets and struggling with how I now felt the community viewed my son's death, and by association, our family. I began to see the online comments, never directed at us, of people making comments about how Narcan shouldn't be free or widely distributed, how addiction was weakness of spirit, judgmental garbage like that. I started to hunker down, brokenhearted in grief and feeling ostracized.

Sam's friends continued to come over, day and night, calling us, texting us, and checking in on Ben. One night one of them let something slip about Silver Lake and "the Tree."

I was sitting at the dinner table, sitting across from her. "What tree?"

The look was one of shock. "You don't know about the tree?"

I looked at Paul, who looked as confused as I did. "No, what tree?"

With a wide smile, and a little embarrassment, the friend told us that the night after Sam's service, a whole group of his friends had climbed the hiking trail to Silver Lake—a place that Sam loved with all his heart—carrying a sapling, water jugs, shovels, and a little bit of mulch. Under the darkening sky as night fell, they planted a tree for Sam at Silver Lake. They'd planted it on state land without permission, but they found a native species, planted it out of the way but easy to get to, made sure it was well watered and mulched, sang his favorite songs, probably drank some, certainly smoked a joint or two, and celebrated their love for Sam in one of his favorite spots in a way they knew he'd approve of.

The thought of that tree helped lift our spirits more than I can say. Trees were a big part of who Sam was. He loved being out in nature any time of year, and he especially loved forests. Friends planting a tree in his memory made so much sense. We wanted to plant a maple tree on our front lawn in his honor, so we understood how important this was to them. Hearing about the tree shook me out of my funk a bit, allowing me to write:

Sunday, November 17, 2013

Friday, I was thankful for being able to spend some time with Amie, and then getting to drive through Addison County on a sunny day. Saturday, I was thankful for living in a place where we can produce so much of our food or get it locally—we had a dinner of salad greens and carrots still coming from our garden topped with our very own cider vinegar, steak from Wagner Ranch, and risotto with our dried tomatoes and kale. Working our land and harvesting our crops helps us keep sane right now. Today, I am thankful for joy-filled memories of Sam. As I have been cleaning out the junk room to return it to being a guest room/TV room, I have found many, many photos, notes, ticket stubs, etc. from Sam—while I admit to shedding a lot of tears today, they were sparked by the memory of the millions of joy and love filled times we all shared.

That night my cousin called, checking to see how I was doing after cleaning out that junk room. He knew that finding those items that triggered memories made me smile, but smile through my sobs. After talking to him, I wrote:

Sunday, November 17, 2013

I am also thankful for my cousin, Ed, who will be embarrassed to be mentioned here in this way—but his constant love, support, humor, guidance, and occasional kicks in the butt over the years, are appre-

ciated more than I can express to him. When I falter, I remember his example, and put one foot in front of the other.

―――――

Around this time, I began to practice what I refer to as "conscious and deliberate gratitude." After Sam's death, I told my father that God and I had "agreed to see other people," meaning that in my grief, I wasn't able to find any connection with a divine force any longer. For years, before God and I broke up, I would get into the car for my forty-five minute commute, and I would pray out loud as I drove down the road. I would talk to God, asking for help and support where I saw it was needed, most often begging for Sam to find his peace, and I would sometimes (not as often as I should have) give thanks. But now, as I was drowning in my own darkness, I began to actively talk out loud as I drove, giving thanks. I guess I was still talking to a divine force of some sort, but in my head, I felt like I was really thanking the universe rather than one divine being. I couldn't follow the rituals of religious prayer, but I could start with expressing gratitude, starting with the parts that were simplest and easiest, giving thanks for Paul and our kids, then later, our grandchild (now grandchildren). I would give thanks for my parents and Paul's parents, people with whom I work, our extended family, and friends. Some days I would openly state that I wanted to be thankful for someone, but I wasn't there on that day. It became an open conversation between my heart/head and the universe.

At first, it was really, really awkward. I'd see another car coming, and I'd stop because I didn't want anyone to see me talking to myself. And I had to remind myself to do this each day. Over time, without really realizing it, it became part of the start of my day. I'd go through the list of things and people for which I was thankful, and it brought a sense of how fortunate I was, even in my darkness. As I tried to do this each morning, I also tried to keep posting about things online.

―――――

Saturday, November 23, 2013

In looking back at this week, it has been a week full of "signs" which have brought some tears, but some laughter too. Monday, I was so thankful for being able to stand and look at our beautiful indoor garden and see that lettuce will be ready to pick soon. Tues-

day, I was thankful for a new Janet Evanovich book arriving—every year I read the new one as soon as it arrives, but this year, it is my special treat for over the coming holiday weekend. Wednesday, I was thankful for Rocky Horror *(soundtrack) being the vehicle of a "sign," and that listening to it really, really loudly on the way home that day, singing along, was the first day without tears during that ride, and I felt a momentary peace. Thursday, I was thankful for the time to sit with Paul in the hot tub and admire the beautiful stars. Friday, I was thankful for the amazing production of "West Side Story" at Otter Valley—being back in a place so full of Sam memories was so hard, but also reminded us of such great times of joy. I was also so thankful to spend some time there with one of Sam's closest friends, and to have my dad be well enough that he could go to the play. Today, I am thankful for the time to go spend some time at holiday bazaars with my mom, and am thankful for the people in Middlebury who didn't pretend they couldn't see us, but instead came up to give us hugs.*

Otter Valley Walking Stick Theater. A daily part of our lives for so many years, OVWST was interwoven through our lives since the day Sam walked into Otter Valley as a seventh grader. Sam had jumped into theater with his whole heart, body, and soul. He did all three rounds of plays (musical, one acts, spring play) every single year.

Here we were, just over a month after Sam's death, and Ben was Officer Krupke in *West Side Story* at Otter Valley. We went to the play, hearts breaking, knowing that Sam had wanted to be there to see Ben perform. We stood in line for the doors to open, standing in front of these folding screens with images from the years of OV plays, image after image of Sam staring us in the face, trying to keep from crying as we stood in the line. No, they weren't there as a tribute to Sam, just a tribute to the incredible performances year after year, but Sam was front and center in so many of those photos. We inched forward in that line, so uncomfortable anyway, hating being in a crowd, trying to not cry as each new photo came into our line of sight. We couldn't close our eyes. We could have asked to have someone save us a seat so we could have just ducked in at the last moment, but that didn't seem right.

Instead, we needed to pull the tiny bit of reserve we had left and stand up straight, make fairly normal conversation, and pray for the anonymity of the darkness of the auditorium.

Finally, we handed over our tickets and went into the auditorium. We struggled to control our breathing as these incredible parents, grandparents, alums, and teachers all came over to talk to us, hug us, and just support us. Lyndsay came to the play, sitting next to us, holding my hand when I started to cry, telling me that she too had experienced a *Rocky Horror* moment the day before, making me believe for the first time, that it might be possible to get "signs" from Sam. I breathed a sigh of relief as the lights dimmed as at least then no one would be able to see my tears. The performance was incredible, as usual, and we made it through better than I would have expected.

Now, normally, we went to one of the four musical performances. For some reason, on that Sunday, we decided unexpectedly to go to the matinee performances, meaning that we would see the play twice. I have to believe that Sam was pushing us to go on that day.

Monday, November 25, 2013

Yesterday was a day of great emotion. I (we) are so very thankful for the very large but close-knit community of the Walking Stick Theater at Otter Valley. We are so thankful for the students and parents who braved their own discomfort to come over and talk to us and to express their support—we know how hard that is. At the end of another amazing, amazing show of West Side Story, we were so touched by the students recognizing Ben for his strength, and for them recognizing Sam. Sam loved that theater program so very much, and we are so thankful to them for recognizing his loss. How blessed we are to be part of that community, and our local community in general!

At the end of each of the runs of a play at Otter Valley, the cast and crew recognize the seniors in the performance with flowers, and honor the directors, Jeff and Ms. Happy. At the end of the performance on that day, Ben's friend Liam stepped to the front of the stage and recognized each of the seniors and the directors, then stood under the lights with flowers still in his hands. In a shaking voice, emotion clouding his always-cheerful face, he said he wanted to recognize one of the actors in the ensemble for his strength during a very difficult time, and he called Ben's name. We stood there with tears streaming down our faces as we watched Ben walk forward and hug Liam, tears running down both of their faces. Liam kept Ben there, and said he also wanted to publicly acknowledge Sam's death, and how important Sam was to the OV theater family. The entire auditorium surged to its feet in a standing ovation as we cried out of grief, gratitude, love, joy, heartache, and so many other emotions. It didn't matter in that moment how he'd died—it mattered that he had *lived*, and these people, all a part of the theater he loved, honored that life.

Following that weekend, my wonderful employers gave me the whole week of Thanksgiving off, knowing how difficult that time was going to be for us. I started working on projects because I needed to stay busy.

Tuesday, November 26, 2013

Today I am thankful for small acts of kindness. We are so thankful for the visits, calls, texts, emails, dinner, brownies, and hugs—hugs are always appreciated. I am also thankful for memories that come from unexpected places. As we have been working on our "junk" room, yesterday I had a moment of laughter as I was emptying out a box from last year's Middlebury Farmers' Market holiday event. Sam had gone to that market to visit and bought fudge from Hannah. After he was done eating all of it and was sprawled out in my chair, he wanted me to go throw the wrapper away. Being mindful that Linnea had warned me once that I might be raising little princes, I told him to get off his butt and throw it away himself. Several rounds of, "Mommy, please? I'm so comfortable..." and me reply-ing, "You're wasting more energy begging than you would walking to the garbage can," ensued. Then I got distracted by a customer, and yesterday, when I got to the bottom of the box, I found that he had tucked the wrapper into a pair of mittens...

This was a perfect example of Sam. He was the nineteen-year-old guy who was not only just willing, but *happy* to go hang out with his mom at Farmers' Market. He would sit, sprawled out in a chair, visit with anyone who came to the booth, wander off to get a snack or check things out, and carry stuff for other vendors, then toward the end of the market, he'd look for ways to trade/barter. He would sit and keep up a running commentary, making me laugh. He was so proud of our fiber/spinning wheel business and wanted to be part of sharing it with the world. Finding that wrapper squirreled away in the mittens made me laugh, then made me cry, then I decided to take it as Sam's way of saying hello.

Wednesday, November 27, 2013

Today I am thankful for having spent the entire day with Paul and Ben, and having talked on the phone with Amie and Ryan (who will both be home tomorrow). I am also so thankful for Paul's example, that even in the midst of hurt and anger, he always shows kindness and does the right thing. I am also thankful for finding the leopard skin outfit picture of Sam and Will today, as that photo just plain fills my heart with light and laughter.

and

Someone has been making little stone towers on Sam's grave, thank you to the mystery builder!

Thursday, November 28, 2013

Today I am thankful for family and friends. My heart aches a little less as I listen to Ben and Ryan playing air hockey, while waiting for my mom and dad and Amie and Jen to arrive. I am thankful for good food, our animals, and living in such a beautiful place. Today, I am also again and again thankful for having had Sam here on earth with us for as long as we did—memories of him fill all of our hearts.

That first Thanksgiving was hell. Sam loved Thanksgiving more than any other holiday. He would start getting hyped up weeks before, all excited to have everyone together for a huge meal. He also had a running bet with his friend Brian, whereby they would each weigh in first thing on Thanksgiving morning, then see how much weight each one of them gained throughout the day, the winner being the one who gained the most. After dinner, he would find the Chipmunks CD and play Christmas songs, like Amie and Ryan had done when they were younger.

Thanksgiving was the first of the major holidays that we had to endure. Paul and I went to the cemetery in the morning and stood together and cried. At the end of the day, we gave thanks for getting through, and for being able to find some moments of relative peace.

Friday, November 29, 2013

Today, I am thankful for "getting through" the first holiday. There were truly beautiful, fun, happy moments, underscored by the sadness. Seeing Amie, Jen, Ben and Ryan together, having Nina and her daughter join us for a bit, having my mom and dad here, all brought joy. How lucky we are to have each other, and to have the amazing support around us. Today, I am also thankful for the stark and glorious beauty of the white snow with the direct sunshine!

We had survived November. Could we survive December?

CHAPTER TWELVE

The December That Almost Broke Us

The problems won't go away
they keep piling on your plate
You just want to escape

When It Rains—Twiddle

I had dreaded the changing of the month on the calendar again. It would be the *second* month without Sam. What I was noticing now was that the shock was beginning to wear off, and overwhelming, crushing grief and sadness were my constant companions. Nothing seemed to bring me much joy, so as I had committed to doing in November, I decided to put an effort into reflecting upon each day and finding *something* for which I was thankful as we went into the new month. It wasn't that I was swimming in joy and thankfulness. It was that by posting, I might not drown in my sorrow.

Sunday, December 1, 2013

Today I am thankful for an incredibly rude supervisor at a store in Middlebury. I was in the store, feeling myself sliding toward a major funk, when waiting in line behind me was the sweetest college student. She didn't have a rewards card for the store, so the clerk asked her supervisor about what to do about the sale prices, and the supervisor yelled across the store that if she didn't have the card, she was out of luck and to charge her full price. Her tone was so harsh that it pushed through the clouds in my brain, and I gave the student my card so she got the sale price. She thanked me four times for my kindness. I am thankful for the rude woman, because she helped me kick myself forward.

Monday, December 2, 2013

Today I am thankful that Linnea is back in the States, and I am so thankful for Sam bringing her into our lives!

I was so thankful as I typed those words. Sam's relationship with Linnea in some ways defied explanation. They'd dated, broken up, been friends, dated, broken up, and remained friends. Regardless of their status, their love and devotion to each other was endless. Linnea being in Bhutan during this time ripped our hearts out because we *all* were so close to her, and we just wanted to hug her in person.

Meanwhile, I went back to work.

Tuesday, December 3, 2013

Today I am thankful for the two women who faithfully guard my office door when I need it, help me laugh, keep me focused, and hand me Kleenex when I need it. Thank you, thank you, thank you.

Then, the dreaded eight-week mark arrived. How silly our marking of time is! Why does eight weeks seem like so much longer than the seven-week mark? But it did, it did.

Wednesday, December 4, 2013

As we have come to the two-month mark, we stop to give thanks again for family and friends who support us each day from both near and far. We also give thanks for each of our four children. We give thanks for Amie's honesty and fierce loyalty. We give thanks for Ryan's humor and humility. We give thanks for Sam's ability to be so forgiving when someone wronged him. We give thanks for Ben's constant kindness and his focus. We ask that if you have children that you take a moment to respond to this post with something you are thankful for about each of your children—because each and every one of them is amazing. If you don't usually post their names, he/she would be just fine. Thank you!

Around this time, I started seeking out other mothers who had lost a child, needing time with them to make me feel less crazy. I wanted so much to be strong and supportive for Paul, just as he was trying to be for me, and at times I just needed to go find one of the moms and howl with sadness or ask them if something was clinically wrong with me, such as a time period when I was going out of my mind with my skin feeling prickly. Hearing other mothers tell me of their experiences made me feel saner.

Thursday, December 5, 2013

Today, I give thanks for a friend who took the time to remind me that while the journey seems overwhelming at times, we can keep going. I appreciate her time and love more that I can express. Today I also give thanks for the life and example of Nelson Mandela. While I have always found him to be an inspiration, today I thought a lot about how three of his own children "departed" before him, and yet he kept going with a message of love and forgiveness.

That Friday, I went to a state meeting for my job, something I'd done so many times before, but for the first time since Sam's death. I was nervous and felt very out of place. Every moment of every day, it felt like my skin didn't fit right anymore, and being there, I felt so awkward. The art of small talk had completely deserted me in the last two months. Luckily, my friend and colleague, Amy, went with me and we met my friend Vicki there. They sat on either side of me throughout the day, steered the conversation so I could participate, and covered for me when I didn't have anything to say.

In the early afternoon, there was a break. I couldn't wait to leave for the day, but I knew I had another 90 minutes before I could duck away. Standing in the hallway with a glass of ice water in my hands, a woman whom I'd known for years came forward, her face creased with sadness. "Kris! I heard you lost your son this fall. I am so sorry to hear that."

Before I could respond, she continued, one hand on my arm. "I know *exactly* what you're going through—I just lost my dog."

Now, don't get me wrong; I *love* my animals. I've held my dear creatures in my arms as they have slipped away from this life, and I have cried buckets for them. But there is no comparison. I'm sure there are people out there who will completely disagree with that, and that's okay, but I bet those who are reading this who have experienced both will agree with me wholeheartedly.

I stood there, shocked, words rushing up, no filter. I hadn't had any sense of a filter since October 9th, and thankfully before I could scream at this very well-intentioned woman, my friends swooped in, almost yelling in unison. "Kris! We need you over here, now!"

Saturday, December 7, 2013

Yesterday I was thankful for Paul being able to spend the day with Amie, and for Vicki and Amy who kept me going yesterday when I would start to falter. How lucky we are to have such wonderful people around us!

and

Today I am thankful for getting to spend some time with Bamby, and for talking with Linnea for a bit. I was also so thankful to hear about the penguin-type bird audition Ben did for the One Act plays. Sam would be so proud!

Just then, a post from an old friend, a friend who had lost her daughter many years before, popped up on my FB feed:

Monday, December 9, 2013

Ohhh, Kristin, so sorry to just now see about Sam. Yours is a journey I wish on no one. I wish, having been there, there was something profound I could say to help. It's a road that you alone must carve out for yourself. Don't let anyone tell you it's right or it's wrong. Let your heart guide you. You are in our thoughts.

That was the first time anyone clearly said to me that my own way of handling this was my right way, and that helped a lot.

Tuesday, December 10, 2013

Yesterday, I was thankful to Sam for bringing Hannah K, Taylor, Emily H, Kirsten and Linnea into our lives. To have such brilliant, beautiful, caring young women in our lives, who reach out in their own ways to support us, is a gift!

Sam had the gift of dating incredible women, women who bring grace, intensity, passion, strength, humor, and acute intelligence to the world. He loved them all (one at a time, of course). In a way that I have never otherwise seen, even after they stopped dating, their deep friendships continued. To this day, those women still inspire and support us.

Around this time, we were invited to go to New York City with Paul's cousin and his family. Marc, Pauline, and their kids had been a constant support—calling, texting, just being there. When they invited us to NYC, we both struggled as we tried to weigh the fact that we felt we *should* go against the question of whether or not we could handle it.

In the meantime, on my own personal front, I'd had an irregular annual checkup because, you know, in the grand scheme of the universe, dumping another round of fear on us was just what we needed. So here we were in the beginning of December, and I had to go in for a uterine biopsy.

A few days after that while we were still waiting for the results, we got on Amtrak and went to New York, probably looking like we were going to the gallows, not Manhattan. On the train, none of us said much, we listened to music, we tried to "get ready" to have fun.

We were just coming into the outer suburbs when my phone signaled a missed call and a voice mail. I guess it was the going in and out of tunnels that caused the hiccup in service. Listening to the voicemail, I heard my doctor's voice. "Kris, I'm trying to reach you. I have the results of your biopsy, and I really would like to talk to you about them today." Okay, when a doctor says they have test results and need to speak to you on that day, you don't immediately jump up and down with joy. You fill with fear, bone-chilling fear.

So that was it. *That* was the breaking point, or so I thought. I immediately whispered to Paul what she had said, and tried to call her back, making sure that Ben didn't know what was going on—thank goodness he had his earbuds in. The call kept being dropped. I kept trying, and kept failing. Each time I couldn't get through, my fear grew.

Just then my phone buzzed again, telling us that we had another voicemail, this one from Amie. Still reeling, I pushed play and the stress in her voice immediately scared me. "Kris, it's me. I just came from the ultrasound and there's a problem. Can you and Dad call me right away, please?"

That moment, sitting on the speeding train, the gray, cloudy weather making the passing scenery echo the grief and despair in my heart, *that* was the moment that I thought I might finally lose my mind, just go into a fetal ball and give up. *How much more could we take?*

In that moment, I remembered how to pray. As I said before, this isn't a book about my religious views, the wonders of Christianity or anything like that, and I had sarcastically told my father in the days right after Sam's death that God and I had decided to see other people. I told him that no one, ever, has prayed as hard as I did for Sam. I prayed for him to find the help he needed, I prayed for him to stop drinking and using drugs, I prayed for him to find his inner peace. And all of those prayers were for *nothing*. The day he died, I totally walked away from the religious beliefs and traditions with which I'd been raised, and hadn't looked back. When I felt thankful for something or someone, I thanked the universe in general.

Now here I was, sitting in this window seat on the train, terrified. Realizing that I didn't have to follow the religious trappings, I thought I could still open my heart and beg a higher power to help us through it all. And I did. I sat in that seat begging for that little baby to be okay. I remember being at a point where I didn't care anywhere near as much as I would have thought about my own health; all of the energy I had was focused on that unborn child.

So we kept trying to call both the doctor and Amie, calls kept being dropped, and we kept trying. Finally getting into NYC, we emerged from the station looking for a bench to sit on so we could call again, sending Ben off to get a hot dog. With shaking hands, I called the doctor again, as Paul used his phone to call Amie. *And the doctor's office had closed for the weekend!*

I got off the phone just as Paul hung up, his face ashen. I took his hand, feeling how cold it was. "What's wrong?"

His voice quivered. "The ultrasound showed something's wrong. They think the baby may be hydrocephalic."

A special educator by trade, I knew what that meant, probably understanding way more than he did at that moment of how bad this could be. First, we'd lost Sam, now we were being told our precious unborn grandchild was in trouble. I tried to keep my voice calm. "Okay. Well, we need to get more information."

He looked at me closely. "What did you find out from the doctor?"

"Nothing. They're closed for the weekend now."

My normally calm and collected husband almost shouted. "Are you kidding me? No, not okay. Call back and ask to talk to the emergency doctor on call. Someone needs to tell us something!" So I did. And I was told that someone would get back to me when they could, as it wasn't an emergency.

We walked the thirty blocks to the apartment where we were going to meet Marc and Pauline, finally telling Ben about the baby. His worry was immediately apparent as he badgered us with questions we couldn't yet answer. Finally, we just focused on walking to the meeting point.

We love to walk in cities, but this was a bit of a hike, and we just kept going, telling Ben we were almost there every single block. When we got to the building, they hadn't arrived yet, so we went to a little pizza place where Ben people watched and made jokes about how Paul couldn't eat spicy food anymore because he was too old. This *boy* knew how stressed we were, and he helped break the tension by keeping up a silly running commentary about passersby. In shock, I realized that was *exactly* what Sam would have done.

Later, we met up with Marc and Pauline and their children, and settled into the borrowed apartment. We called Amie back and had a long conversation, getting as much information as we could, but also hearing that she was going in for so many more tests to find out how bad this was going to be.

Finally, just as we were about to head out to look at the holiday lights, my phone rang. The doctor sounded so apologetic. "Hey, Kris. Sorry you had to wait so long for me to get back to you." Over the next few minutes, she explained that the biopsy showed a rare infection of my uterus. While she couldn't explain how I got it, she could fix it, and my stomach issues should be improved overall. She assured me that she'd already called in the medication, so I could pick it up when we got home the next night.

Phew! One crisis down, and we could now just focus all of our energy on that unborn child, the precious life we had all been so excited about from the first day we heard Amie was pregnant. That little one had become the symbol of hope and life for us all.

Still, here we were in New York, so stressed, so exhausted, but here to have a break with people we adore. We haven't ever felt the need to hide our feelings or anything from Marc and Pauline, so we jumped into the weekend.

Sunday, December 15, 2013

Friday night I was thankful for our (collective) safe travels, and for spending time with Paul, Ben, Nate, Caroline, Pauline and Marc—and for seeingJt Madison Square Garden. Yesterday, I was thankful for seeing The Fantasticks, *great food, laughter and love. I was thankful to Ben for the best moment of theater on the street last night—we laughed more after that than we have in the last two months put together.*

and

And, overall, I am thankful for "signs." Late Friday night, I was struggling with feeling guilty for enjoying my day—I know that sounds stupid if you haven't been through all of this, but it was really bothering me. After a meltdown Friday night, Saturday morning we got on the subway and went to Times Square to get theater tickets. There was a Peruvian group playing in the station and it took my breath away. Years ago, the December after 9/11, we took Sam and Ben to see the Rockettes. After the show, we'd walked back to Times Square to get the tour bus, and Sam heard a Peruvian group playing. In typical Sam fashion, his eyes lit up, and he started dancing around saying it was the most beautiful music he'd ever heard, and begged for the CD. We got it, and it has been a regular in our household ever since. To hear it again, there, brought peace.

――――――

That music brought a moment of searing pain so sharp it took my breath away. The three of us looked at each other in shock, then started to smile. "It's Sam," said Ben. With his words, a tiny bit of peace and light flowed into my heart.

He was right. The fact that music was playing right then, with the memories we had as a family, was a *sign*. Later that night, curled up next to Paul trying to fall asleep I whispered, "That was Sam, wasn't it? He wanted to let us know he's still with us."

"Without a doubt," Paul said.

――――――

Tuesday, December 17, 2013

Yesterday, I was thankful for the breathtaking beauty of the sunshine on the snow. Today, I am thankful for the four amazing children we have raised—over the last few days, we have been told by total strangers/slight acquaintances/old friends how kind and polite all four of our children are. Today, I am especially thankful for and proud of the amazing woman Amie is, how strong, brave, creative, focused and supportive she is—how lucky we are to have her in our lives!

――――――

Each day we waited for updates from Amie, and a lot of them weren't good. There were very real concerns about how severe the brain issues might be; what sort of disabilities our grandchild might face. Through it all, Amie and Jen stayed so upbeat, so calm, saying that we would all, together, face whatever came.

Meanwhile, the blasted holiday season marched on, and with a still-young son, we couldn't pretend Christmas wasn't coming. So, holding back sobs as we returned Sam's Christmas gifts that we'd bought in late September, we tried not to snarl at all the cheerful people we saw.

The last school day before the vacation, I found a small wrapped package on my desk at work. Opening it, I found the book *The Christmas Box* by

Richard Evans, and found a note from a colleague about it meaning a lot to her family.

I walked to the elementary school next door, making my way slowly through the halls to her office. This colleague also was someone with whom I'd gone to high school, and someone who had lost her infant twins years before. After I knocked on her door, she opened it and looked at me and opened her arms, and the two of us hugged and hugged. We sat and talked for a long time, talking in a way we never had before, and she made one of the most perceptive comments anyone had made up to that point in our journey. She told me that she could never understand what it was like to lose a 20-year-old son (hopefully she never will), just like I could never know what it was like to lose infants, so tiny but feisty. While there were differences, the shared experience of losing a child meant that we understood things about each other that others never would. That sameness and difference, that was important to me, and was a thought that I have held on to over the years. And the book? What a beautiful gift, what a beautiful message—to this day, I read it each year at Christmas.

Saturday, December 21, 2013

Wednesday, was thankful for finding out that I "had it in me" to decorate the tree, and it went better than I could have hoped. Thursday, I was thankful for my good friends who not only support me in my odd ideas, they join in and help. Friday morning, I was so thankful for a dream I had. Friday evening, I was thankful for time spent sitting in front of the fire with Paul, talking about our new lives. Today, I am so thankful for my friendship with Nancy and for time spent with Arlie and Hannah, and for the gift that Arlie had made for us.

and

Linnea is home, yay, yay, yay!

Arlie's gift? Arlie and Sam were good friends, and part of it was that Sam could see the wonder in Arlie when many other people struggled to see anything beyond the substance abuse issues and legal problems. Sam saw how smart he is, how talented he is as a chef, how much he loves his children and nieces and nephews. Sam could see past the arrests and the other issues, and see the wonder of him.

On this day, we had gone down to Hannah's farm for a visit and to bring them some holiday gifts. Hannah's son Harper loved Legos and Sam loved Legos, and they loved each other, so we wanted to give Harper a set. After we visited with Harper and Hannah, Arlie came into the living room with a brown paper grocery bag, folded shut, and handed it to us. "I made you this."

I pulled this folded cloth item from the bag, and for a moment I was unsure of what it was. Then I realized it was a tote bag. "Thank you, Arlie."

He came toward us and took the tote bag, opening it up fully. "I found an old pair of Sam's farm shorts in the camper and I knew that you wouldn't probably want them as clothes, so I turned them into a bag, and even kept the pockets because I thought that you might sometimes like to put your hands in Sam's pockets."

This man, who struggled so much in his own life, who had come to Sam's service with his corrections ankle monitor on, had *hand-stitched* a tote bag for us as a gift to not only show his love of Sam, but to comfort us.

Again, I'll say it. *This* was the depth of love that Sam inspired because it was the depth of love he gave. No matter how much our hearts ached with grief, no matter how much the holiday season was beating up on us, that love kept us going.

Then we got hit again.

Tuesday, December 24, 2013

Sadly, our Al passed away today. He was the sweetest, gentlest alpaca, and we will miss him greatly. Today, I am thankful for all the time we got to spend with him, and how much he loved his little herd members. I am also thankful for how incredibly loyal and intuitive alpacas are—their loyalty to their sick buddy brought tears to my eyes.

I love my alpacas. Almost nineteen years ago, I saw an article in the local paper about alpacas. I'd never seen an alpaca, ever. I'd seen llamas, but not alpacas. There was a local farm that allowed families to visit and hang out with their herd for free. So we went. And I met alpacas. And I fell in love. I mean, *LOVE*! They were beautiful, and interesting, and just captured my heart.

For almost two years, we researched, visited farms, put aside little bits of money, and finally bought two alpacas, with a third thrown in as a rescue. There was fluffy white Saber, feeble-but-brilliant-and-loving Chad, and baby Marc. They arrived at our house on a freezing cold January day. We didn't even have a real barn for them, and they moved into our vegetable garden area because it had a rudimentary fence around it.

Over the next months, we (okay, Paul) built a little barn, put up real fencing, and got to know our new friends. And the love affair stayed the same. I just plain loved being with them, watching them, listening to them. Once we sheared them, I learned to spin, and another love was born.

Fast forward to Christmas Eve 2013, to the hell of facing Christmas without Sam, and add in an alpaca who we knew wasn't going to survive. One of the things I've had to learn with our animals is that sometimes medical science can keep something alive but the quality of life is not there, and the kindest thing we can do is give that animal a gentle and painless passing.

Alpacas understand death and sickness in a way that is hard to explain unless you have witnessed it. When an alpaca is getting sick, the others will comfort and support him around the clock, sometimes not eating so their friend is not alone. We have watched them stay awake for hours, keeping a buddy company, and even after death, they will stay with the body and protect it.

When one of our first alpacas died, Paul and I left his body in the barn for a bit while we went to get the tractor, and I had covered his face with a cloth, not wanting to see the open, sightless eyes. When we came back, the cloth had been removed, tossed to the other side of the barn, and the others in the little herd were sitting with the body, their faces touching his. They weren't going to hide from his death, nor hide him, and their understanding of the cycle of life and death has helped shape mine.

Little Al (named Al because Ben always wanted an alpaca named Al), not so small of size, but the youngest of our herd, was struck down by a worm carried by deer. Caught early enough, sometimes an alpaca can survive it, but often they can't. We had tried our best for days, and finally had to admit that we were prolonging his suffering as he could no longer stand or walk.

The vet came. He hadn't heard about Sam, and when he asked where our older son was, and we told him, he stood in the barn and cried with us. Then he prepared to euthanize Al. The other alpacas were laying on either side of Al, humming to him. Sobbing, Paul and I wriggled in between them all, so we could hold Al and talk to him as he left us, knowing he trusted us.

When Al's heart stopped, our oldest alpaca, Marc, rubbed his face against Al's, making a sad, sad sound, then rested his head on Paul's shoulder and gave this comforting sound, like he was trying to comfort *us*. These beautiful animals showed us kindness and empathy in a way we all could understand.

Then, on that Christmas Eve, we took care of the remains, took showers, and dreading it, went to Christmas Eve services because we knew that my parents needed us to be there.

After church, we drove back up over the Bread Loaf Mountain in the inky darkness. Before we had left the house, I had told Paul and Ben that I needed to continue a family tradition that Sam had loved so much.

Many years before, crossing that mountain after church on a Christmas Eve, we had come to the tip-top of the mountain, and in a pull-off there, found a small candle burning, providing a joyous and beautiful light in the pitch black of the night. We had seen it, stopped, lit our church candles, and played Pavarotti's "Ave Maria" in the quiet of the mountain, because Sam loved it, and he was the only one who had a song preference. Sam *always* had a song preference.

Every year after that, we took candles with us so that we could light and leave them after church, listening to the same music as we stood together as a family. That ritual always gave us the sense of wonder and holiness of the holiday, and was so important to the four of us.

Here we were, coming back from church on the first Christmas Eve without Sam, that service where I had cried as the candles were lit at the end and we sang "Oh Holy Night," and I wanted, no, *needed* to stop there at the top of the mountain, light the candles and play "Ave Maria" for Sam. I needed to make a light shine in the darkness so he would know we were thinking of him—to shine a light against the darkness that was in my heart and soul.

Freezing, we stood at that pull-off and lit our candles, tucking them into the snowbank, and turned the music up so loudly that it would reach the heavens so Sam could hear it clearly. The three of us held onto each other in silence, crying, missing Sam so much that we had no words left to express it.

When the song ended, we got in the car and drove home in silence.

We kept that ritual for the next couple of years, as my dad still had a church. Once he retired, we transitioned to lighting candles and leaving them around Sam's maple tree on the front lawn. The first time we lit them at home, the candles burned for more than two nights and days, shining brightly against the darkness.

Wednesday, December 25, 2013

> *Today I am thankful for Paul and Ben, and for my parents, for their understanding, love and support as we all came through our first Christmas in our new lives. I am also thankful for Sbeckles (the cat), who sat on my lap in the sunshine today and kept me company for a while, for Baka (the dog) who almost knocked me over giving me a kiss on our walk, and for Marc and Ellsy (formerly known as Ellsbury) for both giving me nose kisses when I was with them today.*

We got through Christmas—not well, not pretty, but we survived.

Saturday, December 28, 2013

> *On Thursday, I was so thankful that we could spend time with Melissa, my dear friend since the spring of 1976, who also is Ben's madrina (godmother). To have a friend with whom you can sit and laugh and cry and truly express your feelings, is a gift. Then to watch her play air hockey with Ben just plain made me laugh until my sides hurt, which is a welcome feeling.*

and

> *Yesterday, we had so much to be thankful for—first we celebrated our first (belated) family Christmas at Amie and Jen's house. Then, while Paul and I were there, Ben had a visitor at the house—his coach who also had a loss in his family this year, and what an*

incredible gesture of love to have him come check on us. Then Paul and I learned a lot about stereotypes and judging people, when we had the coolest conversation about Dickens-inspired cooking of a Christmas goose with a really unlikely chef—Sam would have loved that conversation! Then, finally, we got to deliver stuff to Outright in Burlington, to help feed homeless teens. This was motivated by the fact that when Sam died, I had already bought all of his Christmas presents—which seemed like rubbing salt in the wounds. We made a family choice that we would use the money that would have gone to those gifts (now returned) to instead help transition-aged youth. So, with help from Patty, we had a carload of stuff to take to Outright, to honor Sam's dedication to treating all people with dignity and equality. Outright was amazing, as Amie had been telling us for years, and my only regret is that it took a tragedy to get me off my butt and get there. While I can't change the past, I can promise I will be there again to help in any way I can.

Sunday, December 29, 2013

Yesterday, I was thankful to share an amazing dinner and a quiet evening in front of the fireplace with Paul. Today, I am thankful for an afternoon spent with Emily and Allie—I wish I had taken the opportunity to get to know Emily better while she was with Sam, but am so thankful for the opportunity now. Again, I will say how absolutely amazing Sam's group of friends is—and how thankful we are that they are still part of our lives.

Monday, December 30, 2013

Today I am thankful for acts of kindness by both strangers and people we have known for years—it was a really hard day, but those acts (or the memory of them) helped.

Tuesday, December 31, 2013

Please forgive the long post—if you have reached your tolerance on my thankfulness posts, I understand it fully. As we have arrived at the last day of the year, we had a conversation that exactly a year ago (after a really rough 2012) we had the conversation that 2013 had to be better than 2012. We sat that evening, and hoped that 2013 would bring health, joy, love and peace to everyone in our family and to our friends near and far. Then 2013 started, and as a family we faced legal issues, health issues, mental health and substance abuse issues, interpersonal issues, and ultimately, Sam's death. But in looking back, 2013 also had some of the most beautiful moments, moments filled with such pure joy, love, and hope. Some of those moments included Sam's pride at getting both the farm internship and later getting the job at the Snow Bowl; Sam's pride at how well his work was going with his psychiatrist; Sam's pride at how good he was at farming; Sam's pride at how well the relationships he had hurt had healed. And there were other amazing moments: Amie announcing her pregnancy and the whole family rejoicing (and Sam's pride that he was the first person in the family to know, and kept the secret for a whole few hours), Ben's theater group going to New England's, our increasing of our farm and loving every moment of it, Ryan recognizing his need to get healthy, Ben's incredible accomplishments at school and outside of school, Dad getting well after a true scare in May, and some health scares for both Paul and I, which all turned out well. As we look back, we too realize again how thankful we are for our local and online communities. The support and love we have received have been truly beyond comprehension—and we hope you all realize how much it means! Please understand this is not a complete list—so please do not be offended if you are not mentioned here. To our friends in and from the Salisbury village, thank you for your constant love and hugs. To Bamby, thank you for always being there—and for crying with us. To Ashton, thank you for your support of us all, and for the gift of kindling for Mormor. To Linnea and Leah, thank you for always being only a couple keyboard clicks away. To Patty and Amy, thank you for keeping me sane and protected. To Cody, thank you for being the first person to reach out your hands to us, and for reading my posts. To Lyndsay, thank you for being part of the family, for crying with me at the play, and for saying it like it is. To

Dot and Royadon, thank you for years of friendship, and being there with us in our new world. To Emily and Vicki, thank you for your check-ins and your very specific remembrances and celebrations of Sam. To Nancy and Jean, thank you for being there and helping me/us feel less crazy. To Sara and Seth and Hannah and John and Harper and Grace, thank you for loving Sam and for your support of us. To Arlie, thank you for your love of Sam, and for your love of us. To Garrett, thank you for your gift of laughter and your support of all of us (the cookie incident in October still makes me laugh). To Taylor, we are so thankful to have you back in our lives. To Emily and Allie, thank you for sharing the hopeful news about many of Sam's friends about whom we had worried so much. To Wendy, thank you for the poem, your support, and the awesome chickens. To Carol, thanks for the messages and your love. To the people of my dad's church, thank you so much for taking such good care of my parents. To Pauline, Marc, Nate and Caroline, thank you for your love and helping us make some new memories. To Ed, thank you for being my emotional barometer. To Lisa and Ralph, thank you for your support, and it is my goal to meet you in person in 2014. To my friends from Middlebury College, thank you for your notes, check-ins, and love. To Will and his family, thank you for your dedication to Sam, and for the visits, treats, and support. To Kirsten, thank you for your check-ins and the musical memories/gifts. To Glenn, I am so glad to have you back in my life. To the Otter Valley Union High School and Leicester Central School community, we cannot thank you enough for your love, support, and understanding. To my school community, I cannot say enough about the support I have received—thank you, thank you. To the people who work at Goodro Lumber, thank you for your support of Paul. To Coach, thank you for showing us how to put good intentions into action. To Outright Vermont, thank you for your support of Vermont teens, and giving us an outlet to help. The list could go on and on, but thank you all—and again, if I forgot to mention you, know we still are thankful for your help and support. And then, I am so thankful to have Paul, Amie, Ryan, Ben and my parents in my life. While we are all in our own grief process, I cannot express adequately how proud I am of my children—they have grown up almost overnight in this process, but they are just plain amazing. I love them, and am so proud of them and thankful to have them in our lives. To Paul, thank you for being my love, my best friend, and my partner in our journey. To my mom and dad, who won't read this because they still don't have a computer, I am so thankful for their constant love and support. And, finally, as 2013 closes, I am, as always, so thankful for Sam. He taught me patience, showed me how to love unconditionally, and to look for new experiences. In the last three months, we have been shoved fully outside our comfort zones, but some of that has brought about new learning, and that is a good thing. Going into a year without him seems daunting, but I know his spirit will be with us, and will help guide us on our journey. Again, thank you all for your love and support. I/we wish you a 2014 full of love, peace, joy, new experiences, opportunities to help others, and new learning. We love you all.

CHAPTER THIRTEEN

The Start of 2014 and the End of Speckles

January 1st, 2014 arrived not in a wave of confetti and joy and excitement, but in a wave of tears and renewed grief. Starting a new year without Sam was even worse than starting a new month without him—he would never experience the year 2014…

Thursday, January 2, 2014

Yesterday, I was thankful for the Boston Red Sox—after a really long, hard day emotionally, watching the DVD of the 2013 World Series was just plain fun.

Saturday, January 4, 2014

Thursday, I was thankful for amazingly good news (more info soon, I promise!). Yesterday, I was thankful for our family—how proud I am of Amie, Jen, Ryan and Ben. Today, I am thankful that my mom's leg is just badly bruised, and not broken, and that I faced one of my deepest fears and made it through.

Oh, that fear… that fear that was almost crippling in its intensity. I was referring to going back to my parents' house. Now, to be realistic, I have some good memories of that house, especially when the kids were little and would go there trick-or-treating, but many of my memories even before Sam's death had to do with my dad's drinking years, so it was a place that I was conflicted about. But after Sam's death? I was absolutely terrified of going into that house, the place where our beautiful boy had died. I avoided it for months, couldn't even think about going there, and suddenly my mom fell and got hurt and I *had* to go get her and take her to the emergency room. I did it, sweating profusely, sick to my stomach, not able to look at the chair where he died, but I did it.

Sunday, January 5, 2014

Today, I am thankful for Sam Z. and Jon— I woke up knowing that today was going to be a hard day, and a note from one and a visit with the other gave me joy and peace. And again, I am thankful to our Sam for bringing them into our lives.

Sundays were—*are*—so hard. Every Sunday afternoon since Paul and I got together, we'd have a nice family meal, then watch a movie together. It was a weekly tradition, and even when Sam went off to college, he often came home on Sundays. When he moved into the apartment, and later the farm, he always came home for Sunday's dinner and a movie. By January, I dreaded Sundays, feeling the need to just get through them.

Monday, January 6, 2014

Okay, now that they finally sent out the news, we can officially say that we are thankful that our amazing granddaughter Sora Aesam was born—and all are doing very well. Proud grandparents are happy to show pictures in person!

Just as 2014 started, in the midst of an awful ice storm, our little miracle baby made her appearance. Yes, there were some issues, but not as severe as we all had expected, and holding that beautiful little baby was a joy beyond description. We cried as we held her, knowing that Uncle Sam would have been the first uncle there to greet her, (he was so very excited to be an uncle) and that she would never meet him, but still holding her made our hearts a little bit lighter.

———

Saturday, January 11, 2014

Tuesday, I was thankful for a really good laugh while doing a Zumba routine. Wednesday, I was thankful for messages from friends and watching Modern Family. Thursday, I was thankful for seeing an old friend unexpectedly. Friday, I was thankful for spending some time with committed and passionate people, then for sharing time and baby pictures with our friend Chad, and sitting in front of the fire with Paul. Today, I am thankful for Arlie and Linnea, both of whom make me smile, and for Ben, who understood why I fell apart over the cell phone issue.

———

Finally, mid-January, I had to face reality about Sam's cell phone. Sam was never going to need a phone again, and for months I had paid the bill because turning it off seemed so *permanent*. I had put it off and put it off. Finally, I had tucked the cell phone (turned off) in a drawer in Sam's desk, not able to look at it or use it, but also not able to deactivate it. Now, I had to face it head-on, and turn it off for good.

Dutifully, I called Verizon and asked to cancel the line. Nope, couldn't do that, we had a contract, we couldn't cancel the account. I argued, not wanting to talk about why, and got nowhere. I asked for a supervisor, and started to cry as I finally told her why I was canceling the line. She couldn't cancel it, but we figured out a way that instead my mom could go on our account for a while, and she helped me to get a new number and order a new phone for my mother—I couldn't have stood for having her use Sam's phone or have her use his number. With shaking hands, I finally pushed the 'confirm' button on the Verizon website, ending Sam's cell contract and setting up my mom's. Then I sat and sobbed, Ben holding my hands as the reality of this hit home. Now, it's almost five years later and I still have Sam's number programmed into my phone, the third phone I've had since he passed. I still have his texts on my phone, and they will be there as long as I can keep transferring them. Of all of the endings in this story, I have to say, cutting off that cell phone seemed one of the most permanent.

Sunday, January 12, 2014

Today I am thankful for being able to spend the whole day with Ben and Paul, and part of the day with Jen, Amie and Sora. I am also thankful for the laughter about toilet paper rolls (what is it about toilet paper rolls and our family?), and for the first time in my life, seeing a shooting star during daylight.

Sunday, January 19, 2014

As I look back at the past week, I am thankful for time spent with Linnea, and our connection to Leah. To sit with Linnea, see the incredible prayer shawl her mom made representing our family, to be able to laugh and cry together, was a gift.

When Linnea came for a visit, the first time we'd seen each other in person since she came back to the United States, there was joy, sorrow, shared grief, and shared memories. She brought with her a prayer shawl that her mom had made for us, where every member of the family was represented by a color, and Sam was represented by sunny yellow—his favorite. The pattern of the shawl represented mountains and rivers (also Sam's favorites), and the color pattern was such that every person was connected to every other, and we all were connected to Sam's yellow. It is a beautiful piece of knitting, created with such pure love, and it has a treasured place in our lives. To this day, when I am feeling especially emotionally fragile, I wear that shawl as emotional support, or maybe as armor.

Sunday, January 19, 2014

As I came to the end of this week, it had been 100 days since "it" happened. I have learned so much in those days. I have learned that love is forever, and that just not seeing someone in person doesn't make you love them any less. I have learned that joy and beauty can shine through darkness, even though I still struggle with it when it happens. I have learned that grief can be both a steady, slow ache, and a visceral and searing pain. I have learned that I can't predict when the sudden sharp pain will hit—when I think something will hit me like a ton of bricks, it may or may not, but then something small will knock me down. I have learned that some extended family members are as integral to my/our life as I expected they would be in a difficult time, and that others, who I would have expected to step forward, are nowhere to be seen (ironically, the really "Christian" relatives are the ones who have gone missing—sorry, snarky comment). I have discovered that some old friends who I would have expected to be there for us aren't, but many, many others have come forward and been constant and loving support for us all. I have discovered that our children have friends who are even more amazing than we knew, and their parents are a huge support for us too. I have learned that I have almost unending patience for some people and situations, and absolutely no patience for other things, such as parents whining about something trivial their kids have done or not done. I have learned that things that once mattered to me, don't, and that new things do, and I have found symbolism in new things that are a comfort to me. In all, I have learned that love matters even more than I fully realized. Love comes in many forms, whether it is a Tree of Life symbol as a gift, a beautiful letter written about a knitting project, friends letting me talk about Sam and crying with me, brownies and bread left on the front steps, a star bracelet to remind me to look to the heavens to talk to Sam, a teen boy carrying Speckles up through the snow so she could get to her food, an orchid blooming in our house, text messages to say someone is thinking of us, Sam's bell ringing at odd times, a quilt for Sora, hugs in the grocery store, and so many other forms. Love is all that matters.

Monday, January 20, 2014

Today I am thankful for having some time to try a couple new recipes, sitting watching the sunset with Paul, and some time with Arlie. And thanks to Arlie for saying that Sam always had a smile on his face.

and

So, everyone has seen/heard many, many MLK Jr. quotes today, but as I struggle to make sense and meaning out of what has happened, I have four that matter to me more now than ever:

"The time is always right to do the right thing."

"Our lives begin to end the day we become silent about things that matter."

"The ultimate measure of a man is not where he stands in moments of comfort, but where he stands at times of challenge and controversy."

"Never succumb to the temptation of bitterness."

Sunday, January 26, 2014

On Tuesday, I was thankful that my new recipes for lunches worked—meaning that I feel more organized in the morning, and less stressed about making sure we are eating properly. Wednesday, I was thankful for time to read a novel for a bit, something I have not done in a while. Thursday, I was thankful for time with some of my past students. Friday, I was thankful for time with my state committee, and for time at Outright Vermont, and for seeing the happiness on my mom's face after meeting Sora in person. Saturday, I was thankful for time spent with Bamby and Cheryl, I am so lucky to have them as friends! Then I was also so thankful for time spent with Carol and Cass, and for the opportunity to pick out our new alpaca, Kahuna. Finally, yesterday, I was thankful for Sbeckles, who mirrored Sam's unconditional love. Today, I am thankful for sunshine, the news that we get to see Pauline and her family soon, and for new recipes again.

and

The cat who would not die, has. RIP Sbeckles (yes, spelled correctly)—you outlived every possible vet prediction, loved Sam and Ben with a passion, and were loyal and loving even after you'd lost your hearing, most of your sight, lost all except one tooth, and had your jaw broken. While I didn't always think I would say this when you were gone, I will miss you, Sbeckie.

That was one of the most painful afternoons I can remember. I had posted the first entry mid-morning, in a better-than-normal mood. Then I went down to feed the alpacas, and found Sbeckie lying in the hay barn, and just seeing her, I knew something was wrong.

Sbeckles came into our lives years before, a tiny barn kitten. She was tiny, smelly, feisty, dumber than a box of rocks even from the beginning, yet Sam and Ben loved that cat. Before her, we'd had really smart, good hunter cats. Not Sbeckie. She couldn't hunt to save her life—why eat a nasty, furry mouse when you can get food in the nice clean bowl? She never really mastered the art of using a litter box, would fall asleep in her bed on the top shelf in the pantry (she used to go there to sleep anyway, so we finally stopped fighting it and just put her bed there), and when the boys would go by and pet her, she would try to purr and then roll out of the bed and go crashing to the floor. She couldn't really purr; she sounded like a faulty lawn mower.

When she was about five or six years old, she displaced her colon. It was one of the grossest things I've ever seen, including when we slaughter our own chickens! We found her outside during a nasty ice storm, her filthy colon dragging behind her. We wrapped her in a blanket and rushed her to the vet. The vet looked at the situation and said that there was very little chance that she would survive the surgery needed, but we had to try—Sam and Ben would never have forgiven us if we didn't. They did the surgery, she survived, and then she ate the stitches holding everything together and it all happened all over again. *Sigh.* Another surgery, a cone around her neck, and she came through it all.

Another couple of years later, she clearly was getting more senile, but was still so loving. Then one day we couldn't find her anywhere, until we found her huddled under the woodshop, barely breathing. Something had attacked her, and had clearly won. Her head was a bloody, pulpy mess, one eye completely closed, her breathing labored.

Off to the vet we went again. The vet found that something had attacked her, broken her jaw, her eye socket, probably a rib or two, and the force of breaking her jaw made her lose many of her teeth. He could stitch up the major gashes, fill her with antibiotics and some pain medication, and she *might* make it. So that's what we did, and she made it through again. A little dumber, clearly deaf in at least one ear, now with only a few teeth, a bit of a limp, and a crooked face. And the cat lived on, still fiercely loving her two boys.

When Sam died, Sbeckie seemed to take on the role of comforting us, even though I fully admit, she often irritated me—I was usually the one who dealt with it when she missed the litter box, or when she would start meowing loudly at random times in the middle of the night, things like that. But she kept trying to support us. She'd follow us up and down the hill to the barns, meowing at us, she'd climb the hay piles to try to bump heads with us, often falling off the bales.

So on the morning I wrote those posts, I had sat with her for a while and all seemed normal, and it was so nice. But later that afternoon, we found her with her colon displaced again, barely alive. Again, with terror in our hearts, we wrapped her in one of Sam's bath towels, tucking one of his felted wool slipper socks next to her, knowing it would still smell of him, and we raced for the vet, needing her to survive because she was a living, breathing link to Sam.

The vet looked at her, and shook his head. "It would be cruel to put her through this again. She might survive the surgery, but not likely, and if she does, she will have no quality of life."

Paul and I looked at each other, tears running down our faces. How could we let her go when she was a link to Sam? How could we make her stay and suffer? With breaking hearts, we agreed it was time to let her go.

Paul held her for a few minutes—this smelly barn cat—and kissed her lumpy head, then told me that he didn't know if he could do it, stay with her when it happened, it hurt too much. I knew that I *needed* to stay with her, I needed to be with her when she crossed over to be with her Sam.

We rearranged her in the towel, putting the sock next to her face, and kissed her and petted her, telling her how much we loved her, and through our sobs, we told her that it was time to go be with Sam; he needed a cat. With a final kiss for that mangy girl, Paul left the room.

She looked up at me through those cloudy eyes, then did the most amazing thing: she wriggled around until she could stick her head in Sam's sock, and started to purr more loudly than I'd ever heard. For the first time in her life, she was actually purring like a cat. The vet gave her the injection, and I told her again and again how Sam was waiting for her and the purring got even louder before it stopped. I know that she knew it was time to go home to Sam, and she was ready; as much as I hated to see her go, I felt peace in that.

Obviously, time has gone on, but I still miss that cat more that I would ever have thought.

———

Tuesday, January 28, 2014

Today, I am thankful for the life of Pete Seeger. Growing up in a pretty hippie household, Seeger, the Guthries, Peter, Paul and Mary and Bob Dylan were the beloved soundtrack to my childhood. Joyfully, it was a love I shared with Sam. I will listen to Seeger again tonight, sing along loudly, and be thankful for his music and his being a role model.

———

Music has been and will always be a constant theme in our journey. Sam loved music, and had music playing all the time, and many times, his deepest and most profound relationships had music attached to them. With Paul, it was their mutual love of America, and their shared trip to see them play—or Alice Cooper, who Sam, Paul, and Ryan went to see together. For me, it was the "hippie" music—the Seegers, Grateful Dead, and more than any other, Arlo Guthrie. When times got tough, we could always get in the car, go for a ride, and listen to Arlo Guthrie together—and he burned at least five CD copies of Arlo's *Can't Help Falling in Love* for me for listening in the car. It didn't matter how rough things were; when Arlo was on the stereo, we could sing along, Sam doing his spot-on imitation.

Pete Seeger's death was sad, but even then, I could realize that my sadness had less to do with an elderly man moving on to his next state of existence, and more to do with another connection to Sam being gone. Truly, it felt as if link after link was disappearing.

CHAPTER FOURTEEN

Tattoos, Rainbows, and a Trip

February 2014 arrived, and we felt the hope of Sora's improvement but still felt so weighted down by the grief and the continuing of the gray, cold winter weather.

Sunday, February 2, 2014

Wednesday, I was thankful for a sign that I was not going crazy. Thursday, I was thankful for great music. Friday, I was thankful for having a phone conversation with Linnea, and for seeing wonderful and caring adults doing great things for kids. Saturday, I was thankful for a call from Hannah that had some great news, and for talking with Amie and making plans with her for a family dinner soon. Today, I am thankful for being able to talk with Ryan for a bit, and for a lazy day to watch movies and football and eat junk food with Ben and Paul. After an interesting conversation this morning, I am also reminded of how thankful I am for my parents—even though they do not always agree with my choices in life, they always, always love me, and are always "in my corner." I was reminded again of how lucky I am to have parents like that—and that they always, always love and support my kids.

and

I try really hard to focus on the positive, and to try to keep putting one foot in front of the other, but having to file federal income tax forms for Sam because of the cancellation of his student loans due to his death is seen as income for him, is just plain wrong and cruel.

––––––––––––

And we again, jumped onto a roller coaster of emotions. Hannah's news? She and John were pregnant with twins, and they wanted to give one of the twins "Sam" as a middle name. Now, we'd known Hannah was pregnant for a while, and in a really strange coincidence, she had found out she was pregnant on the day Sam died, but this news touched us deeply. So of course, I talked to Linnea about this, and she got to laughing, telling me that Sam had told her when Amie announced her pregnancy, that the baby needed to be named after him—he wanted a whole army of little Sams marching around.

Then I had to talk with my parents about something I had avoided for over a month. As I mentioned before, Sam had planned on getting a tattoo on his 21st birthday—he would have gotten it earlier, but frankly, I'd told him that as long as he owed money to Paul and me for his legal bills, he couldn't get one until he was 21. He planned to get a pretty intricate tattoo, but the centerpiece was to be that particular Tree of Life. At the beginning of December, I finally mentioned to Paul that for weeks I'd been thinking about that plan, and I wanted to get the tree tattoo in his memory. I was so shocked when Paul not only supported me in that thought, but said he wanted to do it too.

At the end of December, when we went to Burlington to celebrate a belated Christmas with Amie, we got the tattoos. Now, I do write about it more in a later post, because it was one of the most transformational events of my life, but for right now, just know that I got the tattoo, knowing my parents would be very unhappy about it.

Finally, I got up the nerve to ask them down, saying I needed to tell them something. I told my mom first, her face scrunched up in displeasure, then she looked at it. With a sigh, she told me that it was pretty—for a tattoo. It wasn't a ringing endorsement, but it wasn't a screaming condemnation either—more than I could ever have hoped for.

Then I told my dad. He wanted to see it, so I bared my shoulder, and my father looked at it solemnly. He nodded, then looked me in the eye. "Well. It's well done, I'll give you that."

"Thanks."

"You know I wouldn't have done it."

"I know."

"But you know, I've never walked in your shoes, so I don't have the right to judge."

Again, there wasn't enthusiastic support, but I felt my choice was accepted. Certainly there have been other decisions that I've made that got less parental support. "Thanks, Dad."

Then, after they left, and after having fun watching football with Paul and Ben, I had to finish Sam's taxes. That pushed my buttons more than I can explain. So I wrote that second post.

Within seconds, my Facebook page and my cell phone were blowing up with responses, as friends voiced their support for us. No one trashed the IRS; instead it was all support for us, offers to do the paperwork for us, offers to bring over dinner or just come sit with us. Such love flowed through those messages!

Monday, February 3, 2014

After my frustrations yesterday about the tax stuff, I realized how lucky I am to have all of you in my life—your support means the world, and we love you. Thank you for being with us on this journey!

Wednesday, February 5, 2014

Yesterday, I was thankful for a rainbow in the sky that had absolutely no scientific reason to be there, but spiritually it was in the exact right place at the right time. Today, I am thankful for the beauty of the landscape, and for Lyndsay who is celebrating her birthday today—we love her very much!

Friday, February 7, 2014

Yesterday I was thankful for another rainbow, which I was able to share with Paul. Today, I am thankful for another rainbow, for sunshine, and for looking forward to spending the weekend with a bunch of people I love.

Really, this was when we (family and friends) began to notice the rainbow connection. There had been that very odd rainbow the morning after Sam's service, but suddenly, all of us were beginning to see rainbows at times that made no scientific sense, but they all happened when we were thinking of Sam, and especially when we were struggling. People began posting pictures of the rainbows they saw on Sam's Facebook page and on mine, with little tidbits of why they knew the rainbows were Sam's way of saying hello.

Sunday, February 9, 2014

Yesterday I was thankful for taking the step of visiting the Snow Bowl, and letting myself remember the incredible moments of joy and pride there in regards to all four kids, then let myself feel the sadness too. Then, I had the joy of watching Ben and Caroline come down the Lang, and then watching Ben come down the Allen. Spending the rest of the day with the extended family was a joy, and seeing my father look at his great-granddaughter in person for the first time was a moment beyond description. Last night was filled with laughter, love, and togetherness, as was today. Today, I am thankful for spending the day with Pauline and Marc and Nate and Caroline, and having Ryan come home for a bit.

The Snow Bowl. Middlebury College's Snow Bowl, their downhill ski mountain. All four of our kids learned to ski there—heck, *I* learned to ski there. All three of our boys had worked there as well. It was a part of the fabric of our lives year after year. Sam had been so proud when he earned a full time job (with benefits!) there and was so excited to start that job on October 15th, a day he never got to see.

When winter had arrived, Ben had kept skiing as he had in past years, but I couldn't go to the mountain to watch him; there were too many memories there. When Pauline and family came up and wanted to go skiing, I needed to find the inner strength to go up and see them, and the Bowl. It hurt. I cried, but standing in the sunshine, looking up at that mountain that Sam had loved so much, and Ben still loved, having the workers come up to greet us, it helped bring a little bit of light back into my heart.

Tuesday, February 11, 2014

Yesterday I was thankful for two long phone conversations with Amie, both of which made me laugh, and reminded me of how proud I am of her. Today, after a cranky day, I was so thankful for a package in my mailbox! I thank Sam for bringing Leah into my life—thank you Leah for the treats, the note, and for your love!

Thursday, February 13, 2014

Yesterday I was thankful for being able to spend some time with my knitting, and for good news. Today, I was thankful for a musical good-morning from Sam, when one of the iPods began to play Phish when we had not put it on the playlist...

and

Thank you, Sara. I'm missing him too, and I will never, ever watch the Muppets again without thinking of him.

The second post? A friend of Sam's posted that she was watching the Muppets with her daughter, something they had done so many times with Sam. Yup, the Muppets. How Sam loved them! This was a kid who had a scary intellect; he could read, interpret, and analyze any piece of text, but also always held onto his childlike wonder about things like the Muppets, and wasn't afraid to let others know.

The third week of February arrived, and we were hit by a snow and ice storm. Okay, it's winter in Vermont, this happens. Except that for over a year, we had been planning a trip for the three of us to go to San Francisco, and with the storm, our flights were suddenly canceled, and it looked like the trip might be off. I spent hours on the phone with the travel agent, begging her to find a way to make it work—in my mind, we *needed* that trip. She worked her magic, and off we went, on our first trip without Sam.

Thursday, February 20, 2014

Overheard this morning on a city bus—cheerful bus driver greeted everyone as they entered. Snarky woman says, "What did you win the lottery or something? I've never heard a bus driver be so cheer-ful." Without missing a beat, he said, "I have a choice of waking up each day miserable or with a smile on my face. I choose the smile."

That exchange has stuck with me for years. We got to San Francisco, and I went into an emotional freefall, trying to enjoy being there, loving the time with Ben and Paul, and missing Sam so much I couldn't stand it. Hearing that bus driver gave me a cosmic kick in the butt and made me emotionally recalibrate. I didn't post for the next week—too busy on the trip, trying to process all of the emotions.

Sunday, February 23, 2014

This past week, Paul, Ben and I went to San Francisco. It was a trip we had planned long before Sam's death, but with Sam's knowledge and blessing, it was a trip planned for just the three of us because Sam was supposed to be working at the Snow Bowl. After Sam's death, in my mind, it became a chance to go somewhere where not every single sight, sound, smell would bring a Sam memory—some-place to let my heart and brain be quiet for a bit. In the end, I learned that it doesn't matter where we go, or what we do, there still are Sam memories, or lack of future memories with Sam there. I kept reaching for my phone, to call him and share a moment with him, or to send him a picture. And I can't. But, there were moments where I clearly felt his spirit, and moments when I could feel him urging me/us to be peaceful—and a lot of moments when we said, "Sam would love this place," or "Sam would laugh at that." And, when the Incan musicians started to play at Pier 39, after just hearing a song by America that completely didn't fit with the restaurant play list—those moments brought a smile.

and

Having just posted a long post, I also wanted to add that it was a great trip. We saw the Redwoods, watched the Golden State War-riors, visited Alcatraz, sailed under the Golden Gate Bridge, saw Cirque du Soleil, wandered around Sausalito, ate great meals, and ended our trip with a hotel picnic of amazing sushi, Greek salads, and pizza. We walked in the sunshine on the beach, put our feet in the Pacific, stood under and inside the Redwoods, and watched people. Some moments were touching, some a bit creepy (the guy yelling "Time to meet your maker" on the bus for example), some truly funny. It was a great trip, and I am so thankful that we were able to go, so thankful for Paul and Ben, thankful for Ashton and Bamby helping with the animals—and now it is great to be home.

Monday, February 24, 2014

Okay, so you all know my stand on this issue, but to see that a lob-byist is saying that "We are losing our decency as a nation. Imagine your son being forced to shower with a gay man. That's a horrifying prospect for every mom in the country. What in the world has this nation come to?" offends me to my deepest levels. Not every mom in the country is hate-filled, not every mom teaches her sons and daughters to hate those different from themselves.

Wow! After I posted that, I realized that I was beginning to internalize Sam's message of unending love, and his willingness to stand up for his beliefs. Prior to October 9, 2013, I have to admit that I would never have posted that, even though that was what I felt. But Sam had stood up for his beliefs, working at the local fair to get signatures for the right for gay Vermonters to get married, and had gone to the Vermont State House to hear the testimony. When extended family members made comments about Amie marrying a woman, or said they wouldn't go to the service, he called them out on the need to love everyone and to accept people for who they are. *That* was the moment that I began to realize that Sam had fundamentally changed me through his love, and that I had the responsibility to carry that forward for him.

CHAPTER FIFTEEN

A Cold, Dark March

March arrived, and winter held fast. I kept hoping for an early spring, but the world seemed to be as cold and dark as I felt, and the snow just kept falling. I kept looking for the bits for which I was thankful, and posting about them, although not quite as frequently as before. Frankly, the reality of Sam being gone was sinking in, and it was really hard to remember that there was good, joy, light, and hope in the world right then. So, I would sit with my laptop or iPad and reflect on the time that had passed since my last post and tried to find the positives. I also clearly remember wanting to make sure that the people who were reaching out day after day to support us knew how much it meant to us.

Tuesday, March 4, 2014

Last week was a busy one, in which I was so, so thankful for the incredible people with whom I work. I was also so thankful for getting to see the amazing plays presented by the Walking Stick Theater program at Otter Valley Union High School, spending time with Lyndsay and Jenna, having Ryan, Amie and Jen come home for the weekend, and getting to spend a bunch of time with little Sora. I was also thankful for the teachers, faculty and staff at Otter Valley, who continue to show all of us love and support. This week, I am thankful for family and friends who are there with me/us.

Thursday, March 6, 2014

Yesterday and today, I am thankful for old friends reaching out to us, and thankful for people who knew Sam better than they knew us; reaching out, sharing memories, helping us feel that others hold his memory dear.

Around this time, people started sending us notes, Facebook comments or stopping by to tell us little stories about Sam. Some we knew from him, some were new. Each story told us a little bit more about him and his ability to connect with people.

In the midst of this, one of Sam's best friends (by our and his own determination) made the comment that so many people had posted or said that Sam was "his/her best friend." She said that at first this had made her so angry, because *she* knew she was one of his best friends, and it almost felt like she was being pushed aside. But then she had realized that they were all telling the truth (remember the prologue when I mentioned that perception is reality?) and that Sam had managed to make each of these people feel so special that the words 'best friend' were used. What a gift to be able to make people feel that way!

That reminded me of an episode where I learned a lot about Sam while he was still living. During the last summer of his life, he contracted MRSA. He was working at the farm, his hands were filthy, and he picked at an ingrown hair on his thigh, which then went unnoticed when it got infected, and *shazam!* His leg was swelling, dark stripes around the wound, and when you touched his leg, it was burning up. Off we went to see the doctor on call, who sent us to the emergency room, and they diagnosed MRSA. Wow! MRSA? Sam went through an incredibly painful procedure to clean the wound and had lots of shots (which he absolutely hated). As we were leaving, he ran into a young man with whom he'd gone to grade school. Before I knew it, Sam was sitting down with this man, and asking him about his job, his *multiple* kids (remember, they were just 20 then), and talking about going skiing that winter. This young man was very different from Sam in so many ways, yet the depth of love and respect Sam showed him, and that he gave Sam in return, was incredible. In the car, I waited to hear Sam make a disparaging remark, or say he hadn't meant the ski invitation, but instead he talked about how good it was to see that young man again. Months later, that same young man ran into Ryan, and commented that Sam had been his best friend in his life. And you know what? He was telling the truth.

———

Saturday, March 8, 2014

Today, I am thankful for going into Aubuchon's in Brandon and talking about the Oak Island show, then going to Hannaford in Brandon and seeing several old friends, most especially for seeing Cody. Then, I was thankful for a clean house, a great dinner, and getting ready to plant our seedlings tomorrow.

———

Sunday, March 9, 2014

Today, I am thankful for a long walk in the sunshine, and for having the time to plant our garden seedlings. We planted tomatoes, peppers, cucumbers, cabbage, celery, cilantro, chamomile, basil, swiss chard, kale, broccoli, cauliflower, mustard greens, Brussel sprouts, and a bunch of other things I can't remember. I can't wait to see them sprout!

———

Wednesday, March 12, 2014

Last night, I was thankful for still being able to have a locavore meal: burgers from Wagner Ranch, Vermont cheddar, our home-made hot sauce, our pickles, salad from our indoor garden, salad dressing from our own cider vinegar, and for one member of the family who wanted a slam burger, eggs from our chickens. It was a great meal, and fun (even in the midst of preparing for a huge snowstorm) to be able to enjoy how much is stuff we produced or got nearby.

and

One of the things I have learned in our grief is that things hit at the strangest times. A little while ago, I was looking on Netflix for a movie to watch tonight, and since Sam watched most of the Netflix for the family, recommendations for him keeping coming up. Today, it was a recommendation to watch Boondock Saints, which some of you know was one of his favorite movies—and I got thinking about a trip to the shoe store with him after he'd lost his Crocs in the field, and in typical Sam fashion, he made friends with the store clerk, who happened to be friends with somebody in the movie. That just made his day—and mine, in watching his enthusiasm. Then that day, Ben, Sam and I went out for fish and chips, and the two of them made me laugh until tears ran. So today, I remember with love how much fun we had on that day, and wish he was here in the snowstorm to watch the movie with me/us.

Thursday, March 13, 2014

Late yesterday, I was thankful for laughter when yet another one of my sons looked better in my high heels than I do—and we laughed about the picture here. As always, I am reminded of how comfortable Sam was in his skin, and how much he loved pushing the boundaries of others' comfort levels. No wonder I keep hearing Rocky Horror! *Today, I am thankful for sunshine, all the animals making it safely through the storm, the seedlings sprouting, and that we have a plow!*

One of my favorite pictures of Sam was him dressed in a dress and heels, going to see *Rocky Horror*. He was so comfortable in his own skin!

Sunday, March 16, 2014

Over the last few days, I have been so thankful to have Ryan home with us—and am so excited to have him home for good soon! Yesterday, I was thankful for watching the Otter Valley Walking Stick Theater give an amazing performance of The Birds—and so proud of them for making states. It was an odd feeling to go back to RHS for the performance, our very first visit to that theater was years ago for Blah, Blah, Blah, and it was bittersweet to sit there and enjoy a great performance and wish so much that Samuel M. Francoeur could have been there in body cheering too. Today, I was thankful for a hand reaching out to us in the midst of a difficult day. In a really down moment, I was so thankful for Garrett making me smile—we are so glad to have him as part of our lives!

Monday, March 17, 2014

Today I am thankful for friends who understand and show that hope and joy are possible.

Sunday, March 23, 2014

This weekend, I am thankful for the friendship between Ben and Ashton, thankful that Will stopped by last night (sorry we missed him), thankful to have heard from Arlie yesterday, thankful for the gorgeous sunshine, thankful for spending some time with Paul watching the sunset, and for Bamby who gave us a surprise yes-terday that made me cry—but happy tears. And this week, I am so looking forward to the Vermont One Act Festival at Otter Valley!

and

However, one side note—don't bother telling me you are a Christian if you are going to turn your back on another human being.

The ups and downs. When Ryan came home for a visit in March, he asked if it was okay if he moved in with us. We were so thrilled that he was coming back to Vermont, having been living in New Hampshire for the last several years, and we knew how much he (like the rest of us) was struggling, and knew how much it meant to Ben to have his oldest brother around. Then great moments of school theater brought bittersweet joy. Then my comment about Christians! I began to really openly struggle with my feelings about what I saw as the hypocrisy of many people who claim to be deeply religious. I watched people we knew walk away from their children due to gender or sexual identity; I watched people turn their backs on their children due to their legal issues. But then, I also watched the daily hurt in our own family as members of the extended family who proclaimed their Christian faith acted as if Sam had never even existed, never reached out their hands in support of any of us (even their blood relatives) to offer comfort in any way. I struggled greatly with this (and still do) and hope that at some point I can let go of that hurt and anger. I'm not there yet.

Friday, March 28, 2014

Over the last few days, the grief has been nearer to the surface every moment of the day and night, but through that, I am thankful for the people who serve on my state board with me, the people with whom I work, for the chickens and alpacas who just make me smile all the time, for Linnea always being out there in the universe, for my FB friends who make me feel loved and supported, for the theater program at OV (can't wait to see the performance tonight!), for yarn to knit, for fiber to spin, and for Sora smiling at me today, for Amie, Ben, Ryan and Paul who are just plain amazing, and for the pepper seedlings that are beginning to sprout.

Saturday, March 29, 2014

Today I am thankful for the sunshine, and for getting to see the gorgeous display case at Otter Valley which was paid for with part of the generous donations people made in Sam's memory. It always ticked Sam off to see how little recognition the Walking Stick Theater program got in the big display case, and to see it all proudly displayed now would make him so proud. To look at the pictures of him in Up State, and Blah, Blah, Blah (and other shows) with Sam, Will, Lyndsay, Jenna, Taylor, and so many others made us smile with tears in our eyes. Thank you to all of you in WST who have made such great memories for us over the years!

After Sam's death, money poured in to a fund at Otter Valley in his memory. We had slated the money for the theater program and were thrilled when they used a portion of the money to get a custom display case to showcase their awards. To this day, seeing the case makes me smile for a few seconds before the poignancy of seeing the plaque dedicated to Sam hits.

Monday, March 31, 2014

A friend shared the poem, "She is Gone" by Anonymous with us—it was read by Queen Elizabeth honoring her mother. The friend had shared this with us, changing the pronouns to the masculine form, and I have found myself thinking about it a lot the last few days. Please forgive me sharing the masculine form: "You can shed tears that he is gone, or you can smile because he has lived. You can close your eyes and pray that he'll come back, or you can open your eyes and see all he's left. Your heart can be empty because you can't see him, or you can be full of the love you shared. You can turn your back on tomorrow and live yesterday or you can be happy for tomorrow because of yesterday. You can remember him and only that he's gone, or you can cherish his memory and let it live on. You can cry and close your mind, be empty and turn your back or you can do what he'd want: smile, open your eyes, love and go on."

and

Today, I am thankful for the lessons my children teach me. All four of my children are far more tolerant and accepting than I am, and I have always recognized that about them, and been so thankful for that. Part of my promise to Sam was that I would try to be more like all of them in my acceptance and support of others. Sam's greatest gift, in my mind, was his love of others. As we have said before, he could meet anyone and see something amazing in that person— and he taught us all how to look at others differently. Today, I was reminded again of this as I got to spend time with people that he introduced to us—and I am so thankful for them in our lives.

and

Finally, today I am thankful for the start of the MLB season. It has been the longest, darkest, hardest winter of my life, and since October, I have had one toenail painted green to remind me that spring would eventually come. Seeing the Red Sox play today made me feel like spring actually is on its way!

CHAPTER SIXTEEN

A Resumé, a Crusade, and Spring

April arrived, bringing somewhat better weather. It also brought the upheaval of applying for a new role, replacing my retiring principal. Now, I had hoped for years that when he retired, I would be able to apply to replace him, but really? To apply for a new job *now* was not exactly the best time to try to make a huge professional life change. On top of that, one of Sam's friends gave us some information about Sam that started a chain of events that haunt me to this day. So not knowing who I really was anymore, I tried to put together my professional resumé and apply for a job while I struggled with what to do with this new information.

Sam had run into legal issues with his arrest for DUI. He was ordered probation and a class on substance abuse—yeah, that was *really* helpful for him. Throughout this time, although Sam's conditions of probation said he couldn't drink alcohol (he couldn't anyway due to being underage) or using drugs, he continued with both. Talking to him, threatening him, crying, begging, offering him bribes—nothing worked to stop it. I started telling his probation officer what he was doing. We were so desperate to save him, we felt his going to jail for a while was the best possible option left to us. I called and called, and sent emails—all the time being very open with Sam about what I was doing. Know that trying to turn your own child in is a truly awful, painful, draining thing to do, but we were on a crusade to save his life, and no matter what I said or did, nothing happened. Nothing. I even called his probation officer one day before his appointment, knowing if he was drug tested, at least marijuana would show in his system. *Nothing* happened!

Fast forward to the end of March 2014, and I was lamenting this fact to a friend of Sam's. The look on her face told me there was more to the story, so I pushed. Finally, in a whisper, she told me that the reason nothing had happened was that Sam was doing many of these things with someone close to his PO, and that was why Sam was never held accountable—he knew too much. My hurt and rage were immediate. My child was *dead* due to an overdose, and in my mind, this PO had the power to stop it, and did nothing in order to protect someone who mattered to her. *Finally*, here was the rage people had told me I would feel at some point in my grief. It was here, and it was unstoppable. I wasn't sleeping anyway before I'd learned this, but after? I didn't sleep at all. I lay in bed stewing in my fury.

Over the first few days of April, I sent all of the emails I'd sent to the PO to the head of corrections, along with all my phone contact log information, and what specifics I'd gathered from nagging Sam's friends. I pushed until there was a formal inquiry, and I'm sure I made that PO's life hell—which I would like to think wasn't my intention. I tried to tell myself that I was trying to fix a broken system, but probably deep down, I was really trying to (as hard as this is to admit) inflict as much hurt as I was feeling then. Fast forward to many months after April 2014, and the person who was supposedly doing the partying with Sam was killed in a car accident. I remember sitting and sobbing, ashamed, broken. I had wanted to hold the PO accountable, but I would never, *ever* wish the death of a loved one on any human being.

Back to April 2014, when all that was going on in the background:

Saturday, April 5, 2014

Over the last couple days, I have been thankful to have Ryan home with us for good, for the beginning signs of spring, and for time with family. I also am thankful, so very thankful for Ed, who is turning 50 tomorrow. I know he will be mortified that he is mentioned in a post like this, but since he's in Indiana, he can't do anything about it. Ed has been my cousin, my big-brother figure, my friend, confidante, cheerleader and butt kicker for my entire life. He taught me how to catch frogs, made fun of me for throwing up after too many Shirley Temples, made my kids laugh sticking French fries up his nose and barking like a walrus, took my kids past the "no entry" ropes at the Salem Cross, skied with me, sat and shared more than one pizza in a cemetery as we both learned to accept Mike's death, sang "Grandma got run over by a reindeer" with me many times, called my rabbits the wrong flower names, hiked, swam, walked, biked, took me to the Macy's parade, is there day and night when something is going on with my dad, and got on the first flight out here when he got the call in October. His grace, humor, bravery and perseverance through the difficult moments in his life serve as a daily model for me. His love, support, humor, and butt kicking are appreciated more than I would ever dare express to his face. So, to my cousin Ed, happy early birthday from your dorky cousin—I can't wait to see all of you guys in person in June!

The funny thing? In my confusion about most everything then, I wished Ed a very public happy 50th birthday, when he was actually turning 49. I still get hassled about that mistake!

Tuesday, April 8, 2014

Today I am thankful for the two friends who know me so well that they noticed that my neck had turned red, a sure sign that I was getting emotional about something. I love them and appreciate them more than I can express.

I have really pale skin. Fish-belly white, to be exact. But when I'm emotional? My neck turns steamed lobster red. Streaking, glaring red. Truly attractive, too. I would think I was doing pretty well keeping my emotions under wraps; after all, I wanted to appear sane at work at least. My two protectors at work would look for the signs of a looming meltdown, and spirit me away to safety and privacy. Looking back on that particular day, it wasn't that a big thing happened at work, it was more that as we edged closer and closer to April 9th, my emotions were getting closer and closer to the surface, and I had less and less control over them.

Wednesday, April 9, 2014

Today, we reached the six-month mark. It hit me, us, harder than I could have imagined. While my brain knows that no one day should be harder than the rest, it seems like such a huge milestone. This afternoon, we went to the cemetery, and left some things, and whomever left the Twiddle ticket, thank you. To our mysterious flower deliverer, thank you. Thank you to all of you who visit, it helps us all to know that you have been there. As I look back at the last months, and as I re-read my post from the 100th day, I realize that I am becoming more comfortable in the moments when I find beauty or laughter. Some things still, and probably always will, cause pain so deep that it ties my insides in knots and it is hard to breathe. Some things are mountains that I am trying to climb one at a time, such as making meatloaf this week—but I don't know if I will ever again be able to cook Spam, and I have accepted that some things may be too painful for a really long time or maybe forever. I have learned that my children are stronger, braver, kinder, and more loving than even I thought they were. My husband and our parents are rocks for me, even though they ache as much as I do. Friends have become forever members of the family. My land, garden, and animals help me remember that life continues, and should be celebrated. These months have also shown me unequivocally that there are system flaws in Vermont. We knew of Sam's issues, and tried to get help from every single agency possible. Some were helpful, some not, some caused harm, lots of harm. As I remember Sam, I hold tight to his model of loving everyone and seeing the good in them—and I try to keep that spirit alive in me. But we also are committed to helping bring the issues out into the open, even though that makes some people uncomfortable. One of the things that I have also learned is that it is my firm belief that we need to stop pushing on our children that they need to make us proud, and instead, we need to make our children proud. I firmly believe that Sam would want us to try to make things better for others, and I know we have the support of Amie, Ryan and Ben—and that keeps us going. To all of you, thank you for being there for us in so many ways. Some of you, because of geographical distance, it has been text messages and FB notes, for others, cookies and hugs. For some, it is handing us Kleenex when we need it, for others, not commenting when I say for the 100th time that day that I can't remember who I am supposed to call back. Thank you all for your love, support, and for helping us on our journey. We love you.

Six months. I was shocked to have survived that long.

Monday, April 14, 2014

There are moments when memories sneak up, and when they come to the surface, they hit with almost unbearable pain. Then there are times when the memories seem more like, "Mom, don't take things so seriously," and make me chuckle. This morning was one of those times, when I was on my knees looking for something I had dropped, and I found a dirty bowl and spoon (clearly from ice cream with strawberry sauce) that Sam had left under his bookcase. All the times I squawked at him about putting his dishes in the dishwasher, all the times I have cried wishing I'd spent less time squawking and more time sitting eating ice cream with him, but today, that bowl just made me laugh —he's still leaving dirty dishes for me.

Tuesday, April 15, 2014

Yesterday I was thankful for spending time replanting seedlings into larger pots, seeing things grow is a joy! Then, as those of you who knew Sam personally know, Sam was so very happy and at peace working at Good Earth Farm with Hannah, John and Arlie and Seth and being around his good friends Seth (the other) and Sara (and others) last spring/summer/fall. He loved taking care of the animals and plants, and it brought out a joy in him that was a thing of beauty. For Mothers' Day, Sam brought me four hot pepper seedlings that he had cared for at the farm—proudly telling me that he knew how much I loved making my own hot sauce, and these were hot peppers for me to grow. I made sauce from them last fall, but I also kept seeds (first time I've ever done that) and planted them this spring. Sam's pepper plants are growing well, and they make me smile every time I look at them. Then, as many of you know, he was absolutely enthralled by the garlic he helped grow at the farm—so much so that we decorated both the church for the celebration of his life, and his grave with some heads of the garlic. We took many of the heads of garlic he had helped to raise, and planted them last fall, and when we pulled off the mulch hay yesterday, they are growing!!!!

———————

Each day I would come home from work, make dinner with Paul, we'd eat together as a family, then we'd go check our garden seedlings. No seedlings have *ever* gotten that amount of love and attention.

Then April spring vacation arrived, and we (Paul and I) had to prepare ourselves for another first—15-year-old Ben going away for a couple of days without us. There are no words to express adequately how much of a PTSD response you can have after the death of a child. You become obsessed with the safety of your other children. And poor Ben? As the only one living at home with us for most of the first six months (Ryan had just moved home at this point), he got the brunt of the obsessive worry. I can remember going in to his room after he was asleep, just needing to make sure he was breathing. A small fever? We were almost paralyzed with fear. A year before Sam's death, Ben had a major health scare, which resulted in him being diagnosed with a health condition that worried us all the time for a while. When it made a couple very small appearances? We didn't sleep at *all* those nights.

Now here we were at the vacation, and Linnea had invited Ben to go see her at college. He was going to take the bus all by himself to Boston and meet her, then stay on campus for a few days, and then they were going to get a ride to Lebanon, New Hampshire to meet us. There is no one else on Earth we would have let Ben go stay with at that time, other than Linnea. I don't think I probably would have even agreed to have him go with any blood relatives—just her. We knew she would protect him with the same obsessive ferocity that we would, and that he needed to get away from us for a bit. With shaking hands, we waved goodbye as the bus pulled away.

For hours, we checked our phones almost every five minutes, waiting for the text that he was with her. Finally it arrived, and we could breathe a sigh of relief before we checked into a hotel for a few days alone.

———

Thursday, April 17, 2014

Today, I am thankful that Ben and Linnea get to spend some time together—have fun!

and

Today, as Paul and I walked down Church Street in Burlington, we sat on a bench outside Sweetwater's—and sitting in the sun, I started laughing, telling Paul about going there for a pre-prom dinner, and it was a few minutes of just plain laughter and happy memories.

———

Saturday, April 19, 2014

As I think back on the last week, I am so thankful for the signs of spring, for spending time with Amie, Jen, Sora, Kristen, Linnea, Leah, Ben, Ryan and Paul. The moments of bone-crushing sadness seemed less frequent, until today, when I realized that no matter how much I wanted to honor Sam's love of Jesus Christ Superstar, *I couldn't yet listen to it. Every year, we listened to it together on the day before Easter, getting ready for the holiday. Then, as I knelt in the garden, planting kale and chard seedlings, I remembered how happy he was when we took the boys to see JCS in Springfield, MA, and he'd met the man playing Judas. In typical Sam fashion, he'd sat down with him and had a conversation. Imagine my surprise when he came bursting through the hotel door yelling, "I met Judas! I met Judas!" So while I can't listen yet, I smile remembering the look of absolute joy on his face as he watched the performance, and how at one point in the show, this ox of a boy put his head on my shoulder and squeezed my arm. Even then, that act took my breath away, and even now, remembering it fills me with love and thankfulness for that memory. So, if you have a copy of* Jesus Christ Superstar, *please play a few minutes of it this weekend, loudly, really loudly, so Sam can hear it and know it's for him.*

———

Sunday, April 20, 2014

Today I am thankful for the beautiful sunshine, for getting to hear my dad preach an Easter sermon very much in line with my recent pushing of the idea of accepting a homeless Christ, for sharing a meal with our parents and Ryan and Ben, for watching the seedlings grow, watching the Bruins, and spinning some spring colored fiber. I am also thankful for some time today, sitting by Sam's headstone, playing "Everything's Alright" from Jesus Christ Superstar *really loudly—today, I could listen to it, and feel both the sadness, and the joy he took in listening to it, and feel some lightening of my heart as I did it—I also think he enjoyed the fact that the horses, goats and cows in the pasture nearby all came to the fence to listen appreciatively.*

———

Music, the continued theme. There are so many pieces of music that have great significance; some I could listen to right away, others took more time, and there are still others I haven't been able to listen to yet.

———

Saturday, April 26, 2014

Tirade Alert—this is a tirade, so if you aren't in the mood, skip to the next person's post. Over the last months, I've thought about love and family a lot. A lot. In my darkest moments, I give thanks that the last words Paul, Ben, Mormor, Beepa and I exchanged with Sam were "I love you." Many of you know that my cousin Michael died when I was 13. One of the very few benefits of his death, okay the only one, was that my family finally got the idea that love is not just a feeling, it's an action, and that we needed to both show it and say it. So we say it a lot, and mean it. Will used to hear Sam say it to me at the end of every phone conversation, to a point that he would yell "love you, Mommy" too. But in the last months, we've come to realize that love isn't just for families or romance. There are many of you that I have told I love you over the last months, and I mean it with every ounce of my being—and I'm finally free enough to be able to say it, as well as hopefully, to show you too. But here's the tirade. I do not care if someone in your life/your family has some-

how done you wrong—get off your behind and tell them, write them, text them, whatever, that you care for them. A tiny past issue is not worth being estranged. Very few of us get to know when we will pass, or when our loved ones will, and that stupid little past issue is not worth missing being connected now. I saw an old friend at church on Easter, who has not had contact with her daughter for months because she feels she was wronged. I could barely muster a "Happy Easter" to her, because what I wanted to do was grab her, shake her and yell, "You have a child here with you on this earth, how DARE you not recognize that child, and offer her unending love and support." And that goes for parents, siblings, old friends. If you care for someone, don't let the opportunity pass to tell them. Maybe you aren't ready to walk through their door and hug them, but send a note, or a text, just saying you care. And to all of you, I love you. Thank you for being in our lives. Thank you for being part of our journey, and for letting me have my tirade.

CHAPTER SEVENTEEN

The Trying-To-Be-Merry Month of May

With the start of May 2014, the end-of-the-year craziness began at school. I was in a full-out job search process, complete with multiple interviews for that principalship for which I'd applied, and we had a lot of family events looming large, seeming to eclipse our days.

The first incoming family event was Ben's birthday, in the first week of May. What do you do to celebrate the birth of your youngest when his brother had always made such joyous noise on that day? So, it was Ben's decision to have a relatively quiet family celebration, keeping traditions alive (such as the birthday chair) even as we all tried to pretend there wasn't an empty chair in the room. It was funny—after Sam's death we realized that we had so many family traditions (maybe all families do?), and Sam had been so insistent on observing them each year. For example, late morning on Thanksgiving, we'd have appetizers such as prosciutto puffs, and every year, he'd remind me that I needed to make them because it was a tradition. On Christmas? You started the day with just us as parents with the kids opening the little packages in the stockings, then have a little bit of breakfast, then grandparents came over and we all opened presents (one at a time) youngest to oldest, then had a huge brunch. Traditions/routines were important, and as we went through the firsts and then the seconds and beyond, we've had to wrestle with which ones we have kept, and which we have changed.

The second event was Mothers' Day. The day before, we went to Brandon as we often do to go to Gourmet Provence for a dessert for our date dinner. Paul had already asked what I wanted to do for Mothers' Day, and I had said I wanted the guys to help me redo the flower gardens, then get a pizza. I knew that if I didn't stay as busy as possible, I was going to end up in a fetal position, wailing in my grief. As we got out of the car, we saw a friend walking down the street (the one who told me at Sam's service that it would never get better). After hugs and a round of asking how we each were, she then held one of each of our hands and said, "Mothers' Days and Fathers' Days suck. They just plain suck, no way around it." Her words made me feel so much better—I knew how badly I was dreading that day but felt so ashamed of the feeling. How could I not still be happy on a day celebrating being a mom, when I still had three living, incredible children? How could I just want the whole day to go away? With her words, I knew that I was not the first nor the only grieving parent to feel this way.

Mothers' Day dawned, and I got my first round of crying over with even before I got out of bed. We went to the cemetery, then worked in the garden for hours with the boys. By nightfall, I was exhausted, filthy, but had successfully made it through the day.

Sunday, May 11, 2014

Over the last few days, I have been thankful for an unexpected visit with Kathy, which was greatly needed and appreciated. Then, I was thankful for spending time yesterday with Ben and Garrett before the ball, then for spending time last evening with Linnea and Paul. Today, I was thankful beyond description for having time to sit in the sun with Linnea, then for spending the day with Paul, Ryan and Ben redoing the front gardens, and for getting to spend some time with my mom.

and

Today, and every day, I am thankful for the wonderful moms around me, and for being able to wish Amie and Jen their first official happy mothers' day. I am so thankful for the women out there who are part of our journey—some are with us because of the bonding of a shared journey or experience, and many have not experienced such a loss themselves, but put such love and effort into being there for all of us—and to all of them, thank you, and we love you.

The unexpected thing on Mothers' Day? The absolute deluge of calls, texts, and visits from Sam's friends, coming to wish me a Happy Mothers' Day. Again, these beautiful young people stepped out of their comfort zones to show kindness to someone else, in the name of Sam's love. They have continued this tradition for both Paul and me since then.

Monday, May 12, 2014

Today, I am thankful again to Sam for the amazing people he brought into our lives—and this weekend is the perfect example of that, being able to spend time with Linnea and hearing from Cody. Last night, we had a visit with Michaela and Seth, and are so thankful to have them and their mom, Kimberly and their dad, Mike, in our lives. Sam had the gift of seeing the inherent goodness and beauty in others and bringing them home so we could get to know them too.

The third event was our wedding anniversary, a date which should have just been a simple celebration, now made more meaningful with understanding the depth of our love, and how much we had been through together. Of all the family events, that was the simplest and most joyful to celebrate.

Sunday, May 18, 2014

As I look back at the last week, I am thankful for the news that Amie, Jen and Sora are moving to Rutland—yay!!! I also am thankful for Paul and I celebrating our wedding anniversary—for many years, we have commented that we have had trials and tribulations, but it just made our relationship stronger. There are no words to express how much that is true as I look back at the last 7 months! I am so thankful to have Paul in my life, to have him as the father of our children, and grandfather to Sora. This week, I also was thankful for sunshine, for seeing the garden grow, eating our kale and lettuce straight from the garden, enjoying our new edible-landscaping flower gardens, and seeing the chicks grow. Today, I was thankful, joyful and heartbroken to watch Paul and Amie weed Sam's garlic garden together, with Sora sitting next to them in the stroller. To see them together, with the beautiful garden between them, filled my heart with joy, and then the inescapable heartbreak of missing Sam hit—although, we all felt his presence there with them.

Monday, May 19, 2014

Today, I am thankful for Brian being okay, coming home to find Will visiting with Paul, Ben and Ryan, and then to have Lyndsay come over too. Again, the love we have been shown is nothing short of amazing!

They just kept coming—Sam's friends just kept coming through the door. He'd been gone more than six months, and yet his friends still kept showing up on our doorstep to check on us, to share news of their lives. They checked on Ben day and night through texts and online, keeping an eye on him, giving him attention that was different from our hovering. There were days I'd pull in the driveway from work and find cars there, and Sam's friends on the deck or in the living room.

Saturday, May 24, 2014

Yesterday, I went to my state board meeting, which I look forward to all month long—to have the honor and privilege to work with the most amazing and committed people who put everything they have into helping Vermont's children—that is just plain, a joy. When I got there, though, I heard the news that a friend had lost her beloved son this week—and the news brought tears to my eyes. Then, I turned, and saw this quote ("Everyone deserves a standing ovation once in their lives,") on the white board in the conference room... As those of you who went to Sam's service know, at the end, I asked everyone to give Sam a round of applause, because he truly loved applause, and the applause turned into a raucous standing ovation—and I know Sam heard it and loved it. This quote took my breath away, and I had to take a picture—and I ask all of you to think about when the last time was that you gave someone you love a literal or figurative standing ovation?

and

Today I am thankful for sunshine, a fabulous pedicure, and for going to the Middlebury Farmers' Market. Going to events still is difficult for us, but we are trying more, and today seeing John, Seth, Bob, Hannah, and others was a joy. How lucky we are to have such amazing people in our lives!

———

Sunday, May 25, 2014

As I thought back on yesterday, and how much we enjoyed going to the farmers' market, I also wanted to thank our friend who we saw there, who shared a memory of Sam, about how he had told her about how much her children would like Otter Valley, and she mentioned his name. We talked a lot about that last night, as Paul and I sat on the deck watching first the hummingbirds, then the bats. It is such a gift to us when someone doesn't shy away from mentioning Sam—I know so many people are afraid that mentioning his name will make us sad, but when someone mentions his name, and tells us of a memory of him, it helps so very much.

———

CHAPTER EIGHTEEN

Memorial Activities, Twiddle, and Destruction

A t the end of May, Ben went off to the Hugh O'Brien Youth Leadership seminar, something I fully admit I'd pushed him to do, because I'd done it when I was his age and I'd loved it. We tried not to text too many times to check on him. On the way home, he told us about this amazing speaker, Jamie Utt, and about this song he'd heard and the story behind it, and he wanted us to listen to it.

Monday, June 2, 2014

Thanks to Ben for sharing this song with me ("Clouds" by Zach Sobiak), thanks to Laura for listening with me today, and I really, really like the idea of Sam being up in the clouds where the view's a little nicer.

If you haven't ever listened to this song, do. Truly listen to the words. If you've lost someone you love, I bet you will tear up both in grief, but also in the hope that your loved one has a nicer view.

Sunday, June 8, 2014

It has been a while since I posted some of the things I am thank-ful for—not due to lack of thankfulness, but more from being in a time where the emotions were rolling around a bit more. Over the last two weeks, I have been reminded repeatedly how closely connected absolute joy and happiness are to extreme sadness in missing Sam. So, as I look back on these weeks, I am thankful for friends who sat with me at retirement parties, knowing that I was a bit overwhelmed by the crowd. I am thankful for Ben and his musical choices on the way to school. I am thankful for Carol and her wonderful daughter for bringing Kahuna to us, he is an amazing addition to our little herd. I am thankful for Fluffy, who feels that you should take pleasure when possible, even if you get scolded for it. I am thankful for time spent talking with Ryan, and for his happiness every morning when I hand him breakfast. I am so thankful that Asa Samuel and Hazel June were born safely, and we can't wait to meet the twins in person—Asa has the same long dark hair that Sam did when he was born! I am thankful for watching the garden grow, and being able to go out and pick kale, chard and lettuce every day for dinner. I am thankful for Paul's support as I rattle around sometimes trying to get more comfortable inside myself, and his patience while he is doing the same thing is just amazing. I am thankful for a visit with Nancy and Gail, who make me laugh, and make me feel so loved. I am thankful for Garrett, who not only is an amazing friend to Ben, but is such a joy to have in our lives as well. I am thankful that in a few short weeks, Amie, Jen and Sora will live in Rutland, so much closer than in Burlington! I am thankful for Maureen and Mitchell, who check in on us, and leave surprises on the porch. I am thankful for Cheryl and Bamby, who send check-in texts, and they always seem to know exactly when I need that. I am thankful for OVUHS, and the love and concern the faculty and staff show to Ben. And I am so thankful that the Walking Stick Theater program is going to Scotland next summer (2015) to perform—thinking about that, planning a trip to see Ben perform there, is a wonderfully positive thing for us all. I am thankful that we are able to offer a scholarship at Otter Valley in Sam's name. Sam loved OV, and as we talked it over as a family, we agreed that we wanted to endow a scholarship that was for a student who loves everyone and accepts everyone like

Sam did. While Sam was brilliant, talented, funny, his true gift was in his acceptance of all. Ray Fish presented the scholarship on Thursday night, and his tribute to Sam made our hearts swell—we are so very thankful to him for his words about Sam. The recipient is just the perfect person to receive it! And finally, in remembering that night, I am so thankful that Avery was there, having her sit with us during the presentation was such a help. Phew, that is a lot, sorry for the long post.

The week before that post, Ben had come home from school with incredible news. The Otter Valley theater program had been picked to go to Edinburgh, Scotland to perform in the Fringe Festival—a huge, huge honor. Any theater student who wanted to go, could. Ben wanted to go. Now, we had traveled a lot as a family, but to let him go to Scotland without us? Nope. We weren't there. Really, we tried hard to say it was because we wanted to see them perform, but in the dark of night, we (Paul and I) could admit that we did want to see him perform, but we also couldn't stand the thought of him being that far away without us. I know, I know, it sounds stupid and clingy, but if you haven't lived that fear, you won't understand what was driving us.

We asked Ben, and he actually seemed really happy we wanted to go. Not as chaperones, but as spectators. We would go to Scotland separately from the group, rent an apartment, see the performances, and spend some time with him, but not expect to be with him or the group all the time. We had something for the three of us to look forward to.

We also as a family decided to endow a scholarship fund in Sam's name to be given to a student who wanted to go on to college, and maybe wasn't the most gifted student, but was the type of openhearted, kind, non-judgmental kid Sam was. We put the money into the fund, contacted the school for the logistics, and that June, we awarded the first of them. There was no way we could present it ourselves, but we went to the ceremony and one of Sam's favorite teachers presented it. Thankfully, one of Sam's dearest friends, Avery, was also there to present another scholarship, and she sat with us and held our hands, crying with us when it was awarded.

Then the school year ended. We had made it.

Friday, June 13, 2014

Today, and every day, I am thankful for Ben. Today, he finished his 10th grade of high school, after getting his license yesterday. We always knew that Ben was, and is, amazing, but this year has shown it in ways that we never could have foreseen. He has shown grace, dignity, courage, compassion, kindness, strength, humor, and patience day after day. He has earned amazing grades, played varsity soccer, been in many plays, earned HOBY, worked, played great music for us all, been a role model at school, been an amazing son, brother and uncle, and in it all—always dressed amazingly with amazing hair. Congrats on finishing the school year, Ben, and we are so, so proud of you!

———

At the same time, I was professionally celebrating being named principal of my school for the coming year. I was both excited and terrified but tried to hold on to the pride and excitement. Each day I drove home from school and would make it until I reached one particular hill where I had always either called Sam or he had called me, and I would start to cry. I would cry and cry, then try to pull myself together, listening to music that helped, such as listening to *Rocky Horror* ("Time Warp") and eventually, some Arlo Guthrie or Yanni.

Around the same time, Linnea mentioned that she really wanted to go to a Twiddle show that was near her home, and I reached out to the band because of their connection to Sam (one of his friends had dated a band member, so he'd gone to many of their earliest shows and hung out with them quite a bit). I arranged for Linnea to have a ticket; Paul and I just wanted to give her a moment of joy as she had given us so many times. As I emailed the band, I realized that I needed to work something through on my own. I needed to listen to Twiddle—really listen, because it had been so important to Sam. I was avoiding listening to it because even saying the name hurt. A good friend of Sam's had left a Twiddle ticket stub on his grave, showing how important it was to them as friends, and every time I looked at it I felt I needed to do this for Sam, but it took until June to do so.

On June 14th, I posted a request on Sam's Facebook page for recommendations of Twiddle songs that had mattered to him. In the following hours, his friends posted responses, or texted me with their suggestions. While their list of suggestions went on and on, there were five that appeared over and over in their lists: "Frankenfoote," "Hattibagan McRat," "When it Rains it Poors" (spelled correctly), "Hattie's Jam," and "Syncopated Healing."

So, tears running down my cheeks, I put in my earbuds and started to listen to those five songs while I cleaned the house. I listened to that playlist over and over, catching some of the lyrics, liking the tunes. Then I *really* listened. And I pulled up lyrics, and I read them carefully. Then, over the next weeks, I shared the songs with Paul, and we listened and listened and listened. For a month, we listened. And we *got* it, what Sam had told us over and over and over, that we needed to really hear what Twiddle was telling us.

And we have kept listening, Twiddle somehow forming the underlying soundtrack of our lives.

Sunday, June 15, 2014

On this Fathers' Day, I am most thankful for two dads—my dad and Paul. As those of you who know my dad personally know, our road together has not always been easy, but he has taught me about unconditional love, standing up against injustice, and being there when someone needs you. In these last months, I can't express adequately how much his quiet support, his bravery, his listening ear have meant to me, knowing how much he is grieving on his own. And Paul, when I met him, he was a single dad taking care of two young kids, making sure the kids had everything they needed while he did without. His constant love, support, patience, and guidance are incredible. In these months, I have seen a new side of him, and my love for him, and my admiration of him, grow each day.

and

Today, I also am thankful for the band Twiddle—for the happiness their music brought Sam, and for how they treated Linnea yester-day—there are amazing people in this world, and we are so thankful that so many of them are in our lives!

While still feeling the joy of Linnea's happiness at the concert, we had to face yet another memorial activity, this time at the local elementary school, where the teachers and staff had worked together to buy and set a memorial bench for Sam—a buddy bench where people could just sit together for a bit.

Monday, June 16, 2014

The joy and thankfulness of the memorial activities for Sam are mirrored by the absolute pain and sadness of missing him.

and

(Three photos were posted on my Facebook page and are shared on my author's webpage.) The first photo is one of my all-time favorites of Sam, thanks to Allie for taking it. I loved the picture when she took it years ago, and I love it now even more, because I like to think of him lying on a bench enjoying the sunshine and the clouds. Today, our friends at Leicester Central School honored Sam with a new "buddy bench" near the playground, a place for people to sit and get to know each other. Sam loved LCS with all his heart, knew every inch of the building and the grounds, and especially loved the teachers and staff. It was a place he grew up, loved and protected by all the faculty and staff, with his Mormor always there to keep an eye on him. It was a place he returned to over and over, even after he was long past elementary school. He loved to be there, and to sit and visit with the little kids, happy to get to know them. The new bench is so beautiful, the books they picked to honor him are perfect, and we are so thankful to Sawyer for the wonderful poster on the bench. After the dedication of the bench, we all sang "Sing a Song." Those of you who knew Sam personally know that he loved to sing, wasn't always that good at it, but that never stopped him— he would sing at the top of his lungs filled with joy. To quote the song: Sing, sing a song. Sing out loud, sing out strong, sing of good things not bad. Sing of happy not sad. Sing, sing a song. Make it simple to last your whole life long. Don't worry that it's not good enough for anyone else to hear. Just sing, sing a song. Today, we sang for Sam, not necessarily well, but loud, with love and thanks. So, please sing a song, and at some point, come sit on his buddy bench for a bit.

The summer started. Ben was on vacation, the garden was booming, and suddenly my mom called crying. Someone had desecrated Sam's grave. Shaking with horror and shock, we drove over to see for ourselves—the flower pots had been smashed, the plants ripped from the ground, small memorial items thrown around the cemetery. That all was bad enough, but the person (or persons) responsible had also opened the can of SPAM left in tribute and smeared it all over the headstone. Truly, desecration was not a strong enough word. This was blatant and intentional destruction.

For what seemed like hours, we tried to clean the stone, picking bits of SPAM out of the letters of his name and quote, alternating between crying and being filled with rage. How could someone have done this? This wasn't random. His was the only grave bothered. Was it hatred, or love and despair so deep it came out in this way?

Saturday, June 21, 2014

To the person who desecrated Sam's grave last night, please understand that we understand your hurt, sadness and anger about Sam's death, and we forgive you for what you did, but putting all of us, but especially Sam's Mormor, through finding the grave that way was cruel. We ask that you come to us, own it, and talk with us about what Sam meant to you so that you could act this way. Again, we truly do forgive you, and just ask that you come forward to us.

Monday, June 23, 2014

To the person who vandalized Sam's grave, while several small items are missing, I ask, plead, beg that you return one of them. Sam's Beepa (my dad), who adored Sam as much as Sam adored his Beepa, finally last week put a small cross on the headstone. The cross has incredible sentimental value to Beepa, and it took him more than 8 months of his grieving process to be able to bring it there, and he did it with love. Please, please, please bring back the cross, no questions asked. Please, the act of vandalizing the grave hurt us all, but taking that item has aged my dad so greatly and broken his heart. Please bring it back, please—if you loved Sam, please do it in his honor, give his Beepa back that small token of comfort and caring.

That cross? It was one of my father's favorites. It also was the cross he held in his hands as he offered the last rites to his grandson. That night, whoever desecrated the grave either took or tossed the cross, and it has never been found.

The outpouring of love in response to my posts was amazing. Calls, texts, Facebook posts, and messages all flowed within minutes, with offers of help. We contacted the funeral director to ask about cleaning the stone and found out later that he quietly went there himself several times trying to clean it for us.

The cemetery is a funny place for all of us. Some family members go all the time, some not at all. For me, I go on holidays, birthdays, days when I need to "kick over the bucket of grief." I don't feel Sam's spirit there; I feel it in the garden, the woods, at Silver Lake, in the auditorium at Otter Valley. But for my mom in particular, it is so important that the grave site be cared for and have plants continually. This desecration shook her to her core, and it took a long time for her to come back from it. So, when our wonderful support group asked what they could do to help, I posted the following:

Thursday, June 26, 2014

I posted this yesterday to Sam's feed, but I realized that not all of you see that. We are so thankful for the support of you all—your love, hugs, comments all help so much. Several of you have asked what you can do to help, and I do have a suggestion. My mom, Sam's Mormor, has been the one who has kept beautiful flowers consistently at the grave—but her sadness about the vandalism, and that her pots of flowers were used in the destruction, has made her stop (for right now) putting flowers there. This makes her so sad—it is so important to her that Sam has beauty there just for him. So, if you have wildflowers around, or some extra flowers in your yard (please don't go buy any), we would love it if you brought some there at some point. Please don't put them in containers, in case of another issue. Again, thank you so much for your love and support—we are so lucky to have you all in our lives.

and

To the people who put the sunflowers, daisies, and stone flower at Sam's site, thank you, thank you! My mom called this afternoon, so very happy that someone had done those things—you made her so happy, and I am so grateful for that.

————————

CHAPTER NINETEEN

The First July

July 2014 arrived. July—the month of lots of family birthdays, which were going to be hard enough, but July also marked Sam's 21st birthday. I knew from the moment I woke up on July 1st that it was going to be a long, hard month.

Tuesday, July 1, 2014

Sometimes, when pieces of mail arrive for Sam, it sets me off, and makes me fall apart. Today, after driving home, I was especially fragile, missing him so much. Then, flipping through the mail, a flier had arrived from the Flock Dance Troupe, addressed to Sam, and on the front was the quote, "Life isn't about waiting for the storm to pass, it's about learning to dance in the rain." (Anonymous) I have no doubt that Sam made sure that quote found its way to us today— and if it rains tonight, I'm going outside to dance in it.

and

I realized today that it has been a while since I have posted about those little (and big) things for which I am thankful—it's not because I haven't been thankful, but I fully admit that the last week and a half knocked me around pretty hard emotionally. As I look back over the last couple weeks, I am thankful for friends who are there through thick and thin. I am thankful for beautiful wild flowers and flowers from friends' gardens. I am thankful for our garden and animals, they provide such joy! I am thankful for the opportunity to travel to Rhode Island last weekend, and to spend time with Pauline and her amazing family, and for (finally) getting to meet Harvey, Denise, and Cathy and Madeline—and to see their amazing Mom again. The joy on Paul's face being with all of them was such a wonderful thing. I am thankful for being with Uncle Bob, Paul, Ryan, Ben, Pauline, Nate, Caroline and Marc at the Pawsox, even if hearing "Sweet Caroline" made me cry, thinking of all the times Sam sang it at the top of his lungs, especially the "so good, so good" part. I am thankful for taking a trip with Ryan for the first time in almost 15 years, and for the time to walk on the beaches with him, searching for shells and sea glass. And coming home, today, I am thankful for friends who offered to dance in the rain with me.

———

Wednesday, July 2, 2014

Today, I (finally) listened to "Spamalot" again—first song made my throat tighten, then I sang along and laughed and laughed—Will, I thought of all the times you guys watched, sang, and reenacted Monty Python, and laughed some more. Then it started to rain this afternoon, and yes, I did go dance in the rain. My grandmother, a most amazing woman, taught me to do the Charleston when I was 5 (she was a flapper in the day), and I have taught my kids over the years in her honor. So today, in the pouring rain, I danced the Charleston, and smiled up to them both.

———

Saturday, July 5, 2014

As I look back on the last two days, I am thankful for so many people, things and experiences. Yesterday morning, we had the joy of picking strawberries at Wood's Market Garden—to be able to pick gorgeous, delicious, organic berries right near home, in a spot so beautiful, is a wonderful thing. Then, we went to the Brandon Farmers' Market—Brandon, Vermont and saw friends and just had such a nice time visiting with all of them. Then, we came home, and

I went to visit Kim and we are so thankful to have her and her family as neighbors and friends. Then, last night, Paul and I had a great dinner made from our produce and some other local foods and took a long walk around our land to be thankful for all we have here. Today, we went to the Brandon parade, and saw so many wonderful people, and spent time looking at Kim's fabulous art. Finally, walking back from Kim's, we ran into Gary, who took time from getting to his spot in the parade line-up to tell us that he has figured it out how to fix Sam's gravestone—what kindness he showed! Finally, we talked to Paul's Uncle Bob on the phone tonight—how nice it is to hear his voice.

Sunday, July 13, 2014

Yesterday, I posted a photo quote about the nicest people being covered in tattoos, and I decided it was time to share a memory/story. After Sam's death, I had a thought that kept rolling around inside of me, that I knew Sam planned to get a tattoo around his 21st birthday, and that part of the tattoo was going to have a specific image that was very important to him. Finally, I talked to Paul, and we decided that we were going to get that image in his honor. Let's be realistic, those of you who know us personally really well, can probably imagine how big of a deal that was for us to make the decision, and so unlike the old us. So, at the end of December, we talked to a good friend, asking where she had gotten her tattoos, and we made an appointment, after making sure that Ben was okay with all of this (did he think we'd gone crazy?). We went to Yankee Tattoo in Burlington, scared, uncomfortable, having read every possible article about getting tattoos, how to care for them, how much it might hurt, etc. We went in, and the place was hopping busy, with so many really, really tattooed people, with piercings that we didn't even know were possible, and we sat there waiting, making "We're not in Kansas anymore" comments under our breath, so far out of our comfort zone. Then, they called us in, and the artist got Paul ready, and asked us why we were there, and why we were getting tattoos. We told him, and it was like the world shifted on its axis.

The kindness, interest, and gentleness we experienced there, not just from the artist himself but from the other artists there, was the most mind-blowing experience—we talked about Sam, theater, music, art, love, loss, devastating grief, raising kids, reading Dickens to our children, and so many other things. One of the other artists came in and announced that he had proposed the night before to his male partner, and all these tough-looking guys were hugging him, so excited for them. At the end as we were leaving, there were tears and hugs all around. It truly was a Sam experience—we went with our stereotypes firmly in place and had them knocked over completely. Sam would have loved them all so much—and it is our firm belief that he was proud of us for going through with it. Then, we decided a while later, that we needed to, figuratively speaking, close the circle. We had a memorial tattoo, but we needed one to remind us of why we still get up each day and try to go forward. So, we went back, and again, we walked through the door, and were welcomed like family, with the gentlest concern for how we were, and what could they all do to help. We each got a tattoo that symbolizes for us why we keep going—and as strange as it sounds, it helps. Mine is on my foot, to remind me to keep putting one foot in front of the other. So, that is how Paul and I came to each have two tattoos, one exactly the same, one different but with the same basic meaning. And it you want to know about the images themselves, don't be afraid to ask!

The first tattoos? Sam's Tree of Life from his necklace, with a small star over it because we go outside and talk to the stars to talk to him. The second? For me, I knew I wanted it to symbolize my love for my children and (at the time) my grandchild, to symbolize the love of our family, and the need to put one foot in front of the other no matter how hard it was. Both Paul and I wanted the ohm from Sam's ceremonial prayer flag that Linnea had brought back from Bhutan, and we wanted the same stars that symbolized Sam by the tree in our first tattoos to symbolize the four kids. Paul designed his, but I struggled. So, as I do with a lot of things, I kept asking Sam for a sign of what I was supposed to have in the tattoo. I drew sketch after sketch, but the images weren't giving me any peace. Finally, just days before our appointments, Sam's voice came to me clearly in a dream, his voice joyfully singing one of his favorite songs, the Vermont State Song ("These Green Hills")—and when I awoke, I knew exactly what was supposed to be in that tattoo. Sam loved to sing the line "These green hills, and silver waters, they are my home, they belong to me," at the top of his voice; for some reason, he really liked to sing it in the pool. Anyway, I knew that tattoo was supposed to have one of his favorite spots with the green hills and silver waters, the view from the beach at Branbury State Park. Years later, I still love to look at that tattoo, and it does help remind me to keep going when I am struggling. Side note: Sora knows which star represents her, and will poke at it on my foot when my shoes are off.

Sunday, July 13, 2014

It's been a while since I posted about thankfulness. This week, I was thankful for watching the garden grow, and harvesting beautiful produce. I was thankful for time with Nancy, getting some quieter time with Patty, for being with the parents of the Walking Stick Theater as we plan a fundraiser for Scotland, for seeing Dot at farmers' market, for spending time with Ryan, Ben and Paul, for watching soccer as a family, for seeing Ulti at the store, for eating strawberries from Wood's Market Garden, and for spending time with Fluffy.

Thursday, July 17, 2014

As I look back at the last couple days, I am thankful for the amazing zucchini in the garden and being able to eat food that we grow. I'm thankful for going to the Billings Farm Museum (finally) with Ben, Isabelle, Amie, Sora and Paul, and having fun there, then going to Sculpturefest in Woodstock—so cool! I am thankful for time with Ryan and Kim, for watching all the produce grow in the garden, for a great dinner at Bove's last night with Paul, then sitting watching the sunset over Lake Champlain, and seeing a rainbow. Now, as dinner cooks, I am thankful for the wonderful smells of our onions, garlic, basil, oregano, zucchini, yellow squash and tomatoes from Woods cooking.

and

And, I am thankful today for a few (far too short) minutes with Melissa, who isn't on Facebook, but after 39 years of friendship, we can still pick up a conversation mid-sentence, laugh and cry together. How lucky I am to have her in our lives!

Saturday, July 19, 2014

Warning—this is a tirade. In watching the absolutely heartbreaking news out of the Ukraine over the last days, I have come to realize that part of the "new me" is how painfully strongly I feel for others who have lost loved ones, especially their children—I always cared, but now, my heart aches for those families in their first hours/days of loss. To see that just now are investigators/rescue workers being let in with limited access, to gather the remains is unacceptable. To put those families through knowing that their babies, husbands, wives, parents, friends are strewn over fields and not being recovered and treated with the respect they deserve is barbarity even in a war zone.

and

This is the flip side of my tirade, as I know how easy it would be to slip just into negativity. Yesterday, I was thankful for the Brandon Farmers' Market and a little visit with Dot (and her amazing bread), for seeing Bob, for visiting with Ryan and Kim and getting to see more of Kim's art, for visiting with Hannah and Hazel and Asa, for turning around and seeing Cody and getting to visit with him and to finally meet Carter, and then for suddenly seeing Amie, Jen and Sora. I am so thankful for the look of joy and love on Cody's face as I introduced him to Sora, and for his understanding of why she has a tie-dyed shirt, and for his comment about guardian angels. Today, I am thankful for seeing Joanne and seeing her joy talking about spending the day with her grandchildren, and for seeing our old friend Olivia. Then, I was thankful for an encounter with someone who Sam didn't really like that much, who stopped me to tell me how sorry that person was for his death, and how kind and pleasant Sam had always been. My heart swelled with pride hearing someone who wasn't one of Sam's buddies still say how well he still treated that person. Finally, I am thankful for Ryan and Ben, who just plain are amazing, and I am so proud of them.

Monday, July 21, 2014

Today, I am thankful for my husband, Paul. It is his birthday, and as I have been thinking about the symbolism of birthdays, I realize that there are so many reasons to be thankful for him. When we met in 1991, I was so young, stubborn, opinionated, scared, insecure, the list goes on and on. He saw through that, and stuck with me/us. When we met, he was a single dad, who would have done anything to protect and care for Amie and Ryan, often sacrificing greatly himself to make sure they had anything they needed/wanted. He patiently held my hand through my first months/years of motherhood, helping me understand parenting, and the weirdness of sibling relationships (as an only child myself). He showed me courage in challenging stereotypes, such as being the stay-at-home parent when Ben was born, and for loving and supporting all the kids through ups and downs that would break many parents. In these last months, I have learned even more about the depth and strength of his character/soul, watching him in moments of unfathomable grief and sadness, and moments of great joy. I have watched him put his thoughts/feelings into action, even when others might think him/us "weird." I have always liked the phrase "moral compass," and Paul's compass is as true north as it can be, following his beliefs of honesty, kindness, and above all, love. So, to my husband, happy birthday, and I love you more than I can express.

After Paul's birthday, we had to face the coming of Sam's birthday. It had been on all of our minds almost constantly for a couple of weeks, and so we finally sat down together to decide what to do to mark that day.

Tuesday, July 22, 2014

As a family, we have spent a lot of time discussing Sam's upcoming birthday. No matter how much we miss him, we choose to remember

July 30th with our absolute joy and love in his arrival on this earth. Therefore, we would like to invite all of you to join us in a celebration of all our love for Sam, and for the joy he brought us all, and for all of us to have a chance to see each other again. We invite you to join us for a cook-out at Branbury State Park on Lake Dunmore at 5 p.m. on July 30th. (A rain site will be circulated at a later date.) We will provide hot dogs, hummus, chips, soda/water, some produce, and some kind of dessert. If you have something in abundance in your garden or farm, or a recipe that you know Sam loved, please feel free to bring it, but you don't need to bring anything but yourself. It costs $3.00 to enter the park, but please, if that is a problem for you, just tell them that you are with the Francoeurs. Please bring musical instruments if you like to play them, Frisbees, balls, lawn chairs if you want, towels, swimsuits if you want to swim, and great memories of Sam to share. We have a couple "rules." Please come prepared to introduce yourself to someone there you don't know, as we all know that Sam never saw anyone as a stranger, everyone was a friend he had not yet met. Also, we ask that there be absolutely no alcohol or drugs, and that you not use before you arrive—please respect that many members of our new extended "Sam family" are in recovery. We hope that you can join us on July 30th! Please RSVP by email or Facebook by July 29th so we know how much food to bring.

———————

Saturday, July 26, 2014

Today I am thankful for so many things. First, I am so thankful for the response to our invitation to the celebration on Wednesday—wow! Then, I went into the Middlebury Farmers' Market, and got to visit with great people, got some amazing moussaka for everyone for lunch. Then, after lunch, we harvested some lettuce, Swiss chard, 20 cucumbers, 15 squash, beets, three huge heads of broccoli, onions and celery—some of each will be in our dinner tonight. Then we picked our blueberries and raspberries, and the first foraged blackberries of the season. Finally, we harvested our garlic, and I am so very thankful for our garlic. As many of you know, we planted the garlic last fall from heads that Sam had helped care for at the farm, and he loved the garlic. We made a garlic bed, and have fussed over it since, the symbolism of it never far from our minds. Then, this spring, Marc the alpaca decided to break out of the fence and roll around in the garlic bed, and we were heartbroken and worried. Hannah told us not to worry, that it would be okay. She was right! Today we harvested the most beautiful heads of garlic—they are curing now, and some of them will be saved to replant for next year. I fully admit to tearing up several times as we harvested—and I am so thankful for the bountiful harvest.

In reading back over my posts, this one reminded me of a truly awful day early in the spring of 2014, which I hadn't posted about because I was trying to find the positives to share. There was one day when Paul and I realized that Marc, our oldest alpaca, was out on the lawn. Not okay. If everything was the way it should be on our farm, they would pretty much always be in their fenced area. Not only was Marc out, but the other alpacas as well. We watched in horror as we ran down the hill toward Marc with a bucket of grain as a bribe to get him back in the pasture. He ran over to the garlic beds, jumped the fence, and rolled in the garlic. I mean *rolled*. Legs in the air, full big body squashing down these proud, healthy plants. And in our panic, we suddenly realized that he clearly had already rolled in the other box too. Screaming, we got him out of the garlic, and chased all three back into their pen, then walked back up the hill to look at the garlic boxes.

I thought that might be the day that Paul and I just plain gave up. We had put so much love into the garlic, and when Marc rolled in it and squashed it flat, it went from this incredibly healthy and happy looking plot to a disaster, and every time we walked by it, a little hunk of our hearts was ripped out again. We hadn't been able to protect Sam, and now, we had even failed to protect his garlic!

When we looked at the squashed garlic, we cried. We stood on the lawn, and cried. No, "cry" does not adequately describe what we did. Ultimately we knelt on the ground, holding onto each other and sobbed, and I remember needing to wipe my nose on my shirt, snot was running so freely. All the while, Marc stood at the fence, clearly not understanding why we were so upset. After all, he'd gotten out before and gotten into things like the pumpkin patch, and we'd never acted that way before.

When the tears stopped, we talked about ripping it all up, because clearly it was destroyed. In desperation, we decided that we would call two farming experts in our lives, hoping for good news about whether the garlic would survive. The first coldly told us that the garlic was probably ruined. The second said it would be fine, and for us to relax. She said that regardless of how the greenery looked, the heads would be fine. Thankfully, she was the one who was right! Just before Sam's birthday, we carefully harvested our first crop of Sam's garlic, and miracle of miracle, every single clove we had planted had grown. We had counted how many we planted, and we counted the heads, and it was a perfect match. Not all were huge, and some were a bit funny looking, but they all grew. Sam's garlic grew!

Tuesday, July 29, 2014

To answer the question just posted to me privately, anyone and everyone is invited to the Celebration at Branbury tomorrow night at 5 p.m. While it is on Sam's birthday, it is neither a birthday party nor a memorial service—it is a gathering of friends (new and old) and family, to celebrate the amazing power of love and joy, and to celebrate our amazing community. You don't need to have known Sam, or know us particularly well, just want to enjoy the company of amazing people, and share a meal together. If you play an instrument, bring it—you all know that Mormor will get us singing at some point!

Late the night of July 30th, we got home, so tired and so thankful. We'd spent the evening with so many people who love us and love Sam. We'd eaten, laughed, cried, and watched little ones swim in the lake. People sang, old friends found each other, and new friendships were made. After putting away the leftovers at home and taking showers, Paul and I climbed into bed to watch some mindless television while we decompressed from the day. Finally, we curled up and fell asleep, feeling that we had more than survived Sam's birthday, that we had celebrated love being triumphant.

At almost midnight, we were awakened by the phone ringing next to my ear. The room was so dark, so cool with the air conditioner, that when the phone woke me, I was completely disoriented, then terrified.

"Hello?"

"Kris? It's me. I needed to call and tell you something."

"Okay." At this point, I had absolutely no clue who was on the phone, especially since I didn't look at the caller ID when I answered it (not that it would have probably helped that much).

"I was driving home today, crossing the bridge, and the most beautiful rainbow crossed the sky, and I knew it was Sam, saying hello. And I knew that he wanted me to tell you that."

As the conversation progressed, I realized who was calling, calling all the way from Portland, Oregon, and with the time difference, it was still light there. "I could feel it, Kris. I could feel Sam telling me that I needed to call you and tell you he loves you. It was his birthday message to you guys."

I started to cry. "Thank you."

"Thank Sam. I just paid attention." With words of love, she hung up.

Afterwards, we sat in bed, and realized she was right. Sam had found a way to make sure that his message got to us.

———

Thursday, July 31, 2014

There are not enough words in the English language to express our thankfulness to all of you who joined us in person or in spirit in our celebration last night. It was truly a "Sam Night"—great weather, great people, lots of food. To those who could not join us in person, thank you for your notes, calls, and positive thoughts. It was a gorgeous night, and the combination of people brought joy and love to us—thank you, thank you. Thanks to so many people who joined us. It was so much fun to see people reconnect, or meet for the first time, and to see new friendships formed. We love you all, and are so thankful that you are in our lives.

———

CHAPTER TWENTY

A New Job, Another Loss, and Trees

With the start of August, I tried to hold onto the idea that we had made it through Sam's birthday, which had to be one of the hardest firsts yet. I also tried to wrap my head around the idea that I was now the principal of one of the largest middle schools in the state of Vermont, and I tried to look like I knew what I was doing. I was trying as hard as I could to keep all the balls in the air, trying to survive each day.

Every day I got up and went to work, thankful for my job, and thankful for the support of the people with whom I worked. Their support, humor, and patience kept me going professionally. When I got home, Paul and I would head outside to take care of the animals and work in the garden, and that digging in the soil, pulling the weeds, harvesting the bounty, helped. It was in the garden, touching the earth, that I could most feel Sam's spirit, and felt most connected with him. I continued to try to post regularly in my conscious and deliberate gratitude, and over and over, the themes of the incredible people in our lives, the wonders of gardening, and our animals repeated themselves. Those were the parts of my life that brought moments of joy or moments of peace—sometimes both.

Monday, August 4, 2014

Yesterday, I was thankful for playing with Sora, driving to Shore-
ham to get Ben, laughing with Ben and Paul, picking almost 2 gal-

lons of blackberries, and making a pasta salad with our zucchini, onions, peppers, tomatoes, cucumbers, beets and celery. Today, I am thankful that our solar panels have gone online (yay, yay, yay), and am thankful for a dinner of our tomato sauce, roast chicken that we raised, our sautéed Swiss chard, onions and garlic, and that Fluffy is finally coming out of molting, so her mood is improving, and her new feathers are beautiful.

Poor Fluffy. She was such an incredibly sweet and loving chicken. But when she molted? She became this cranky, not-so-bright bird. She looked disgusting; bare chicken skin is not attractive, and she looked lopsided when she walked. She wouldn't lay an egg for weeks when molting, and would sit, broody, in the nest until we kicked her out of it each day. When she would come out of molting, she would be especially friendly, as if to apologize for how she acted in the weeks before.

Sunday, August 17, 2014

It has been a while since I wrote about being thankful. That is due to the combination of two different factors. First, it has been a very busy couple of weeks. Second, it has been a couple of weeks with large amounts of sadness, grief, exhaustion, and stress. I admit that it has been harder than usual to find the moments of beauty and wonder, and much easier to slip into darker moods. Having said that, there still have been moments of beauty and wonder that have taken my breath away. First, we are so thankful for Avery, who came by the house recently with one of the most thoughtful gifts we have ever been given, and even as I write this, thinking of it fills my eyes with tears of love. We are also thankful to Barron and Muffie, Kirsten and Avery for sharing the photos/videos of their wish lanterns with us. We are thankful for our garden, which not only provides us with food, we (Paul and I) find the closest thing to peace when we work in the garden. I am thankful to Patty for always being the quiet support around me. I am thankful for Mike for making Paul so happy in reading his note. I am thankful for the Little League World Series, which brings joy and laughter to our household—and I so love how

excited we get about the standings there. I am thankful for the amaz-
ing people with whom I work, who constantly show me how much
they love our students. I am thankful for Bamby and Cheryl, who
are the best at the text check-ins, which help keep me grounded. The
news that Arlie is doing well and is back around this area made me
sit and cry tears of joy. I am thankful for the joy on Ryan's face at
his family birthday party today—how thankful we are to have him
back around, and so healthy now. I am thankful for the phone call
yesterday from Tatiana, which came at a very dark moment for me,
and by the end of the conversation, I was filled again with how lucky
we are to have the friends and family we have. I am thankful for the
music of Arlo Guthrie. Yesterday, I heard Amazing Grace *sung at*
a mass, beautifully, but so formally/flowery. Always I am thankful
for the music of Arlo Guthrie. Sam always loved the Arlo version
of the song, and the last time I had heard it, was at his service.
Yesterday, I sat and played the Arlo version for him, and let the
beauty of his arrangement fill my soul. Finally, after spending most
of Friday night at Rutland Hospital with my dad being very ill, I am
thankful that his surgery today went very well, and that he should
heal well—and I am thankful for Paul's constant support and help
through everything.

In the middle of August, one of the students in my school committed suicide. It was the second death of a student our school had suffered in a couple
of years, and it almost broke us as a school community. Here we were, still
on summer break supposedly, and we needed to mobilize to support our students and faculty through this loss. I would like to say I led it well. I think I
probably bungled it at lot, still so raw in my own grief over Sam, and so sad
about the death of the student that I think I probably mishandled some parts.

The worst moment in her death and the aftermath? When the Catholic
priest called out her parents at the funeral, telling their surviving children that
since she hadn't been baptized, Heaven was in doubt. I almost lost my mind
then, sitting in the middle of a row so I couldn't leave the service even as I
could feel it getting harder and harder to breathe, trying to understand how
anyone could say such a thing to a room full of grieving children.

After her funeral, I sat on Sam's grave and played the Arlo Guthrie version of "Amazing Grace" for him, and cried, and sang along. And it helped. Then I drove home, still so raw, and when I parked the car at home, there was a group of OV football players there, talking with Ben and Paul as they collected bottles for a fundraiser, and without stopping to think about what I was doing, I confronted one of the players who had lost his sister several years before, and asked him how he would have felt if a priest had said something like that at her service. I remember the immediate shock and hurt on his face, not hurt because I'd asked, but hurt for the girl who had died and for her family. He hugged me, something he'd never done before, and said that was an unforgivable thing for any priest to say. How right he was!

Several days later, with the permission of my boss, I called the priest to confront him about his comment, and to explain how his remarks had reverberated through my students, as they questioned their own possibility of entering Heaven. His response was that he stood by his actions; that by saying that maybe other children in the room would make their parents get them baptized. He said he was doing what God would want him to do. If that's how God sees things, that the action (or lack of action) on the part of a parent excludes the child from Heaven, that isn't a god I want to follow.

The gift mentioned that meant so much? Trees. Lots of trees. Sam has a friend who, on his birthday each year, gives the number of trees of his age to the Arbor Day Foundation. To date, more than 80 trees have been planted. Sam loved trees, loved to be in the trees, and the idea that the forests are being replanted in his name gives us peace and joy.

Reaching Out

With the start of September (or the end of August really), the school year really began. I was thrust into my new professional role with a school community still reeling from the loss of a student. Every morning I summoned the strength to try to be there for my students, faculty and staff, not sure how I could help them in their grief while I was still so broken myself. I would try to find my inner strength both professionally and personally, but woke each day knowing that October 9th was coming, and I had no choice but to get through that anniversary date. Here it was, more than a month before, and I was already dreading it every minute of every day.

As September started, and as the weeks went on, I found myself slipping into a deeper funk. I think it was the combination of the coming anniversary, and the wearing off of the shock. The cold, permanent reality began to set in. For months, I'd been so raw, so inundated by details and things that needed to be handled, that I was in a fog. Now the fog was lifting, but the melancholy was pretty deep-rooted, and I needed to actively work on breaking out of it before it took over, seemingly for good.

Thursday, September 4, 2014

Today was a rough day for many reasons, but as I drove home, I realized that I was focusing far too much on the negatives, and that

I was moving away from recognizing the joys in our lives. With that in mind, I am thankful that over the last couple weeks, we have been able to spend some time with Will and Linnea, enjoyed eggplants from plants from Mitch, had a "random act of baked goods," and we have watched Ben play some amazing soccer (even injured). We have kayaked on Fern Lake, spent some time with Bamby, canned and frozen and dried our produce, and have played with Sora. We have spent time with Arlie and are so thankful for his progress. We have realized we are stronger than we realized in terms of our inner strength doing some needed things on our farm. We have reconnected with old friends like Mike and Sean, both of whom make us laugh—for which we are so thankful. We have enjoyed seeing how much electricity our solar panels have produced, something that Sam always hoped we would do. At the end of the day, I am so thankful to the people around us, who show us every day how much they care, and how kind and loving they are.

Wednesday, September 10, 2014

Today was a day that kicked me around the block several times, and then firmly reminded me of the blessings in our lives. Every morning, for just a moment as I wake up, I can think that the last eleven months have been a dream, and that I will find Sam sound asleep on the couch, snoring, when I come down the stairs. Then, each morning, there is the crushing reality that is not the case. Almost all mornings (after the first month or so), I have been able to get up, and put one foot in front of the other (hence the tattoo on my foot), and found joy and beauty in the day, even in my grief. Today, I couldn't shake it. I cried on my way to work, which I usually don't do, listened to Sam's favorite songs trying to find some joy and peace, didn't, and had to force myself forward. Then, I sent out a plea to some of Sam's friends, asking for a happy, love-filled or silly memory or picture, to help me remember the smiles, not the sadness. There are not enough words to describe the thankfulness I have for Linnea, Lyndsay, Taylor and Kirsten. They not only answered my plea, they gave me new images or glimpses of Sam—

and also showed me once again how lucky we are that Sam brought them into our lives. A friend recently commented about what wonderful people we have around us, and she is so, so right.

———

When I put that plea on Sam's page, I needed help, badly. I had been able to usually push myself forward and keep busy enough to break through the wall when I was really falling apart. But this day? I couldn't. I was wallowing in the grief, and I couldn't remember anything but the pain and loss. All my normal techniques for getting out of the hole didn't work, so I asked for help—and as people did every time, I reached out from the darkness, and they responded. Those four young women, and so many other friends, sent memories of Sam that made me smile. And it helped so much.

———

Thursday, September 11, 2014

Today was a day filled with much lighter than yesterday, and more peace—in great part due to all of your amazing support. Thank you all!

———

Sunday, September 14, 2014

As I look back at the last three days, there have been so many great moments. Friday, sitting in the sun at the OV soccer game, listening to Garrett yell at the top of his lungs was a joy, as was seeing Larry, who is a constant support for us all. Saturday and Sunday, spending time with Pauline and her family just filled the house with laughter and love. Watching Ben, Ryan, Paul, Aunt Pauline, Claire, Marc, Pauline, Nate and Caroline press cider made me smile.

———

That Hated October

October arrived. I really hate October. October will forever be the month when Sam died, and no matter how beautiful the foliage, or how much I enjoy the weather or fall events, I hate October.

October 2014 arrived, and I felt the weight of every passing moment, each one leading to the dreaded anniversary.

Thursday, October 2, 2014

I have a so-so relationship with poetry. There are poems, and poets, that I greatly enjoy (especially anything by Ferlinghetti) and a lot that I don't. But, this morning, someone shared the recently released epic poem by Edward Hirsch, dedicated to his son Gabriel who died several years ago. The second stanza took my breath away: "I did not know the work of mourning Is like carrying a bag of cement Up a mountain at night The mountaintop is not in sight Because there is no mountaintop Poor Sisyphus grief I did not know I would struggle Through a ragged underbrush Without an upward path Because there is no path There is only a blunt rock With a river to fall into And Time with its medieval chambers Time with its jagged edges And blunt instruments I did not know the work of mourning Is a labor in the dark We carry deep inside ourselves Though sometimes when I sleep I am with him again And then I wake Poor Sisyphus grief I am not ready for your heaviness Cemented to my body Look closely and you will see Almost everyone carrying bags Of cement on their shoulders That's why it takes courage To get out of bed in the morning And climb into the day."

and

After sharing the poem, which some of you may see as a sign that today was a hard day, well, it was. Truthfully, "good" days are hard, bad days are almost unbearable. This morning, I woke with the bags of cement Hirsch references seeming heavier than normal. Then, we had a FB message from Garrett which lifted the sadness so dramatically. We are so, so thankful to have him in our lives. Then, later, I got to see Karen, who I had not seen in a while. The few minutes with her made me smile, and feel comforted, and what a gift that was!

Then we reached "the" week. How do you pretend that you are okay when that date is marching ever closer? How can you keep going when all you want to do is crawl into a ball for a bit, and just mourn—not cook, clean, work, take care of others, make small talk, do anything? How can you still be there for each other in the family, when you know everyone else is struggling too?

Sunday, October 5, 2014

Several people have asked us what they can do to help us as we go into this especially emotion-laden week. The answer is simple, do something with your child/sibling/parent that they have been asking you to do with them, and you have just kept saying "I'll get around to it later." Do it now, with joy and love, and appreciate the opportunity to do so.

Tuesday, October 7, 2014

Tomorrow morning, there is a lunar eclipse which (if the sky is clear) we should be able to see. The symbolism of the light of the moon being hidden, then revealed again, seems so appropriate right now. Feeling so deep in the darkness right now, I hope it symbolizes coming lighter days.

Thursday, October 9, 2014

Last night, the skies around Leicester and Brandon glowed with the most beautiful rainbows—and as many of you know Sam's life and afterlife have been full of rainbows. For all of us, the rainbows brought beauty, and some peace.

and

Many of you have heard us talk about Sam's love of music, and many of you have commented on how often he listened to music or sang—always at the top of his lungs. In his honor, we are listening to a playlist of songs that make us think of him. Please feel free to add some others that you think should be here.

The Vermont State Song
SpongeBob—"Best Day Ever"
Jesus Christ Superstar—"Everything's Alright"
Bob Dylan—"Like a Rolling Stone"
Arlo Guthrie—"Motorcycle Song"
Twiddle—"When it Rains it Poors"
Twiddle—"Hattibagan McRat"
Zach Sobiak—"Clouds"
America—"Horse with No Name"
Aerosmith—"Amazing"
Rocky Horror—"Time Warp"
Macklemore—"Same Love"
Tom Petty—"Into the Great Wide Open"
Andrea Bocelli—"Por Ti Volare"
Pavarotti—"Ave Maria"
Bryan Adams—"I will Always Return"
Arlo Guthrie—"Amazing Grace"

and

Today, we want to thank all of you for your amazing love, sup-port, patience, humor, understanding, protecting, behind the scenes orchestrating, filling in for us, feeding us, taking care of our extended family, and more than anything, thank you for your love of, and helping us keep Sam's memory alive. We love you all!

and

When we saw Arlo perform at the Paramount not that long ago, Sam made me promise that when Arlo went out on this tour, I would take him. I promised. And we will go to whatever venue is closest, and I know Sam's spirit will be there, and probably will be at every other performance too.

That final post came, when in a moment of cosmic, universal coincidence, Arlo Guthrie publically announced that he would be going on tour with "Alice's Restaurant"—something Sam had listened to with us more times than we could count, and we had promised him if Arlo ever went on tour again doing it, we would take him. On October 9, 2014—Arlo announced the tour. Seriously, Sam, really? It was if Sam was making sure we knew he was still with us.

That first anniversary was spent in the way we all individually needed to spend it. We hiked to Silver Lake and checked on Sam's tree. We planted garlic with friends and family. Sam's friends stopped by the house or called or texted. We went to the cemetery. We cried, we laughed, and we reminisced.

At some point, I took time to read posts on Sam's Facebook page. While I'm not including the entire posts, here a just a few of the quotes that hit me the hardest or made the most impact:

I miss knowing that there was someone who understood me to the fullest extent—my highs, lows, moods—and would never judge or sever our friendship. There are so many things that I would love to relive. I'd love to hear you talk to your mother on the phone—always ending with an "I love you." I'd love to put you in the passenger seat of the Subaru and go for a ride. I'd love to listen to "It wasn't me," "Mr. Bojangles," and anything by SOJA while you sing at the top of your lungs. If I had one more opportunity to be annoyed by your rendition of The Magic Flute, it wouldn't be enough. If I could watch our friendship grow over the past 15 years again, it would still be too short. I want one more deep conversation, one more hug, one more laugh, one more adventure, one more sunset, one more walk, one more smoke. I want to tell you how much you mean to me, and how much I love you because I didn't say it enough. You were, and always will be, my best friend and I miss you one million times around the solar system. All my love.

———

I miss seeing you walking down the road, offering you a ride, but knowing you'd rather walk with nature and freedom. I miss your smile, your laugh, your jokes, and your presence. Most of all, I miss the love and light you brought into this world and am so grateful for the time we were able to spend together.

———

I miss the excitement and appreciation you had for the simplest things. Whether it was inviting you to visit me at school, making you dinner after working on the farm, you were always thrilled by life's simplest pleasures, and you enjoyed the experience of just being more than anyone I have ever met. You savored life and new experiences, and that energy was infectious. There isn't a day that goes by where I don't think "Sam would have loved this", or "Sam would have thought this was hilarious" or, mainly "Sam would make this situation so much better." There's no means to put into words all the ways that I miss you, but every day I see life through a different, more embracing, more joyful lens because you're always here with me to open my eyes.

———

A year ago today, the world lost a ray of sunshine in a cold, dark place. Sam was a son, a brother, a friend. He was a lover-of-the-outdoors, a student, an entrepreneur of extremely tasteful music, a movie watcher, and an outgoing spirit. He was a shoulder to cry on, and an ear to listen. He was a guide of all the beauty the world has to offer. Sometimes it's hard to find the beauty in things when such horrible things happen, but you keep your head up, sing a little louder, and dance.

———

One year ago today, the world lost the brightest light. While we're merely in different rooms of life right now, the loss that we all feel is fresh. We miss your love, your laughter, and your life every day.

Today marks a year since a beautiful, joyous light was extinguished from the world too soon. Sam was an active and eager participant in all that life had to offer, and he reached so many people, in so many different ways. Perhaps his most wonderful and far-reaching quality was his love of laughter, fun, and a good time. Even in the worst situations, Sam was there to find some humor, lightness and beauty. Today I woke up, confused, very sad and ready to write a somber post. I tried to put on Pandora, and, of course, my music froze on 80's hits: "the safety dance" by Men Without Hats. There Sam was, reminding me to lighten up and find the happy in life.

One year ago today. I miss you randomly showing up in my life at the most necessary times. I miss seeing you walking around, barefoot most of the time, with nothing but a backpack full of findings. I miss drives home after play practice way back during high school days when all of our lives were carefree. Your laugh, your stories, your amazing outlook on life and the list goes on. I am grateful to have known such an amazing person and I am so happy to see that your memory lives on.

There's not a day that goes by that I don't miss you Sam. I can't thank you enough for all the beautiful sunsets and rainbows over the past year, and for sending me perhaps the last monarch in Vermont this morning when I needed it most. We carry your smile, your laugh, and your love for life with us every day. You left us all with such beautiful, funny memories, ones that make us proud to have called you a friend. We dedicate our pursuit to love unconditionally to you Sam, rest easy Captain, see you around

---

It's been a long year Sam. It's not easy being without one of my brothers this long. You showed me what accepting others was all about. Your genuine love for all people was shown to me the first time I met you as little kids as you came up to me that first day of 2nd grade and said, "Hi, I'm Sam and we're gonna be best friends."

One year ago... I can't believe it. I see you every day in the sunset and in the moon shining through the clouds. I see you this autumn as the color climbs up the mountains and in every rainbow smiling down at us. I miss you bud.

More than anything else, we felt the love—the love we shared/share with Sam, the love we have been shown by the community, the love he inspired. And we survived the day.

After hours and hours of discussion, we had decided to plant a maple tree for Sam on our lawn. We decided we would plant a maple tree because Sam had always wanted us to return to sugaring. We went to so many nurseries, trying to find the perfect tree, without success. Finally, we'd asked a friend because she'd planted a beautiful one in her father's memory, so I thought she might be able to suggest a place to buy one. I asked her, and she looked at me like I was a complete idiot. In amusement, she said, "We hiked into the swamp and dug one up. Why would you buy one?"

So that's what we did. Paul, Ryan, Ben, and I dug up a maple tree from our pasture, Ryan dug the biggest, deepest hole to plant it in, we put special items in the hole, and planted the tree.

Friday, October 24, 2014

We had wanted to plant a tree at our house that would be Sam's tree, and now it is planted, and supported. No tree has ever been loved as much as this one, and if love and care can help a tree take roots, this one will!

Like the garlic, every ounce of our love went into planting this tree, seeing it symbolizing Sam and our love for him. We planted that tree so carefully, and have babied it every day since, and it is growing and growing, and all of us love to be around Sam's tree—if you want to see the tree's growth and progress, I regularly post photos of it on my author's webpage.

CHAPTER TWENTY-THREE

The Ups and Downs of November and December

A s November 2014 began, I was posting with less frequency as I struggled, not wanting to admit it. I was also facing some major health challenges, but other than Paul and my doctors (and the boys to a lesser degree) we tried to keep it pretty quiet. Looking back from my current vantage point, I can see how my health issues were impacting every moment of every day.

Sunday, November 2, 2014

(Long post, sorry.) A couple weeks ago, right before my birthday, someone who hates to be mentioned here but knows me better than most, asked the question of whether my relative FB silence was because I was so busy/doing well, or because I was struggling so badly that I couldn't find the warm fuzzies anymore. I thought a lot about that, a lot. After getting through my birthday, it sort of gelled in my head, and I realized what was going on. As we approached the one-year mark, I kept hoping/expecting/begging that on day 366, the "light" would come back on for me/us. I felt that once I had gotten through the first year of "firsts" that it would be easier to bear. As my birthday came closer, and then passed, I realized that the seconds may be harder sometimes than the firsts, and as I can't change this, I need to learn to accept it the best I can. Having said that,

that same person said that what I/we needed to do was to see the moments of joy and celebrate them. I knew that before, but I really needed the reminder. This person has always been good at giving me a swift kick when I need it, for which I am (and always have been) grateful. So, in looking for the moments of joy and beauty, I have a bunch to share. First, I am thankful for the joy with which Ben's soccer team played this year, and how awesome the parents/ grandparents were. I am thankful to Avery for long ago leaving Sam some Twiddle ticket stubs which nudged me into listening to Twiddle, which I do every day now. I am thankful for Sam's friends who leave little things for him, and I find great comfort in seeing them, and knowing the love with which they were left. I am thankful for friends who ask us how we are, and really want to hear the answer. I am thankful for conversations with friends where we can laugh until it hurts to breathe (thanks, Kristen!) I am thankful for the OV football team for giving us something absolutely fun to do on Saturdays, and thankful for Nancy and dancing. I am thankful for friends like Sue who are helping lead the Brandon Cares charge. I am thankful for Lyndsay and Linnea who are always there for us. I am thankful for Hamjob and know how proud and pleased Sam would be for them. I am thankful for Fluffy the chicken, who is always pleased to see us. I am thankful for the enthusiasm with which Ellsbury eats the celery plants when we pull them from the garden. I am thankful for time with Paul, Ben, Amie, Jen, Sora and Ryan, and for spending more time lately with my parents. I am thankful for an amazing conversation at the cemetery with another member of this lousy club. I am thankful that whomever took the pumpkins from Sam's grave took them, instead of smashing them—it gave us the hope that someone was enjoying carving them, maybe while thinking of Sam. I am thankful for the garden, which still is producing an abundance of produce for us. I am thankful to live in a place that is so beautiful, and where nature is all around us. I am thankful for the wild turkeys who visit us regularly. And finally, I am thankful to the person who asked the question and made me reflect for a bit.

Stuff at the cemetery. Lots of stuff. The first couple days after Sam was buried, there were flowers at the grave. But once his stone was put in place, stuff started appearing. Little towers of stacked stones. An empty box of Marlboros (the brand he'd smoked), a Frisbee showing his love of Ultimate, a couple of crystals that caught the light and made rainbows, pennies, little gnomes, a can of SPAM, shells, sea glass, hockey memorabilia—it all appeared (and continues to) showing that people were thinking of him and making the trip to visit his resting place and leave a memento. Sometimes things appear only to leave again, but often come back. It's all a bit of a mystery.

There are members of our extended family who felt uncomfortable with the tokens, and felt that some of them, like the cigarette box, were somehow disrespectful, but our immediate family felt that we didn't have the right to ban any gifts—these weren't for us, they were for Sam, and he would never have turned anyone away. These little tokens speak volumes about the love he gave and inspired.

I leave tokens too. When I got my first official business cards as a writer, I went right over with a laminated one and left it for Sam. When we go to the ocean, I bring back sea glass for him because searching for it was something we loved to do together—and besides, something broken that is battered around until it is soft and beautiful? I like the symbolism.

Then someone posted this on my Facebook page:

————

Sunday, November 9, 2014

I met a high schooler who was visiting Wheaton last night who recognized me from senior year States in Scapin. When I asked him what show he was in, he told me, and I immediately remembered watching it with Sam. He immediately then said "Man, you and that show Upstate—You guys were amazing. They totally should have gone on too!" and our conversation quickly switched to the OV Theater department to which he immediately said "Do you know the blonde kid from Upstate? He was so frickin cool." Sam is everywhere, and I love it.

————

Sam was living on through complete strangers, and what a gift that was to us all! It wasn't only people close to him who were keeping his memory alive, but complete strangers as well.

Sunday, November 16, 2014

Lately, due to a lot of things, I have been falling into the pattern of "growing a garden of grievances." People driving stupidly (but not dangerously) irritate me more than they should, the coffee maker dying made me almost cry, the fact that our garden has almost reached the end of its season makes me sad instead of proud of how long we have kept it going, and the list went on and on. I kept trying to kick myself out of the mood, with little success. Over the last couple days, it began to lift, and I was able to remember and see the beauty around me. We stood outside in the cold last night and looked at the Milky Way. Today, we worked together on putting the garden to bed for the winter and listened to the alpacas happily munch on the things we pulled up. I reconnected with a good friend who makes me laugh, thanks Tess! We got to see both Emily and Cody today, and again, I give thanks to Sam for bringing the most awesome people into our lives. Today, I got to listen to Paul and Ben irritate each other with an ice scraper, which made me laugh. We enjoyed a meal of chicken we raised, with our leeks, spaghetti squash, garlic, beets, celery and carrots, all picked today, and now chicken soup is boiling on the stove with a pot of spaghetti sauce next to it—again, all things we produced. I sat and spun some gorgeous alpaca yarn while watching football. And suddenly, the mood lifted completely. So, as we reach the end of the day today, I am thankful for the wonders, big and small, around me.

Sometimes I needed to post things on Sam's Facebook page, like I was talking to him directly.

Wednesday, November 19, 2014

Some days I just plain miss your joyful noises—noises about everything, everyone and everywhere. I miss how excited you were about everything.

Then we started to get ready for Thanksgiving, and I found it even more overwhelming during this, the second Thanksgiving, than the first.

***

Wednesday, November 26, 2014

As we prepare for Thanksgiving this year, I am finding it harder even than last year—maybe last year the shock was still too fresh, and I so strongly felt the need to show that I could get through it. This year, it feels like being in slow motion. That's not to say there are almost an infinite number of things to be thankful for, it's just that they are harder to see right now. But, one thing is abundantly clear, being able to spend the day with Ryan, Paul and Ben today was a true joy!

and

One of the things I struggled with today was the memory of Sam and Brian having their annual contest to see who could gain the most weight on Thanksgiving. Sam's excitement every Thanksgiving Eve, as he would write himself a reminder to weigh himself at his "emptiest" point, was just plain funny to watch—it was a tradition. Then, as soon as he had eaten so, so much, he would go weigh himself. I have no idea how many times each one of them won, but it always brought a lot of laughter to our house. Sam loved every part of Thanksgiving, often saying it was his favorite holiday by far, but the silly contest was a favorite part for him—and finally late this afternoon I could laugh thinking of it. To Brian and his family, we send our love and thanks for the laughter over the years—we hope your Thanksgiving is full of love and laughter and a lot of mashed potatoes.

***

With Sam gone, those silly traditions seemed even more precious, and on the second Thanksgiving, it hurt even more than the first, which both surprised and scared me. If I'd thought the "seconds" would be easier, and instead they were harder, how would I ever make it through the "thirds" and beyond?

***

Sunday, November 30, 2014

As the Thanksgiving weekend comes to an end, I spent some time today reflecting on the last few days. Last Wednesday was a joy from start to finish, spending time with Ryan, Paul and Ben. Thursday was difficult pretty much from start to finish. The joys of being with loved ones was overshadowed by the gigantic hole in our midst—made even larger by how much Sam loved Thanksgiving and how committed he was to the "traditions." I guess the reality is that I was so convinced that since we had gotten through last Thanksgiving pretty well, that this one would be easier. Maybe last year it was that the shock also kept the pain somewhat subdued. This year, it was so raw and ever present, and at moments it was hard to breathe, let alone remember to be thankful for the wonders in our lives. Today, we took some time to relax, and Paul, Ryan, Ben and I went to the movies— we rarely go to the movies, and the last time Ryan went with us was many years ago—what a treat to be together. Now, after another meal of leftovers, the guys are watching the Patriots, and it is so cool to hear them chattering away. So, in looking back, it strikes me again how many wonders we have in our lives, and once again, I lost sight of that for a bit. First, we have wonderful people in our lives, like Lyndsay (great pie!) and Will (great rolls!) and so many others. We have relatives and friends who call, text, stop by, send messages, etc.—their love keeps us going. We have the wonderful music that Sam loved so much, which we listen to and can feel his presence. We live in a beautiful place. We have our families, friends, great jobs, wonderful animals, great vegetables growing in the house and in the greenhouse, fiber to spin, yarn to knit, and love, lots of love.

Suddenly and shockingly, my health issues went from being constant and chronic to nearing a crisis level. One day at work, I was struck down with what would later be labeled as a thunderclap migraine, causing me to pass out. I was taken by ambulance to the hospital, and then there were days and days of tests and fear as they tried to figure everything out.

One of the side effects of the time in the hospital was that when I had a lumbar puncture, it didn't seal up properly, and I had debilitating headaches for almost two weeks. In this time, I kept being sent back to the emergency room for more and more tests. And the stress got worse, I needed more care, and I was less and less able to handle the stresses of it all coming together.

Thursday, December 4, 2014

I don't say this enough, but Paul is just plain amazing. I am thankful beyond expression for his love, patience, sense of humor and devotion.

Tuesday, December 9, 2014

Yesterday, we encountered one of the most unpleasant persons I have ever met. We met this person in the midst of a very stressful time, in a stressful place, and he was in a position of power and authority. His blatant disrespect, condescension, and lack of compassion was appalling. When my temper cooled (let me be clear that I was ripping mad) I realized that if this schmuck was treating us this way, thinking he was so all-high-and-mighty educated, etc., how would he treat someone with a disability, someone poor, frightened, vulnerable? As I thought about this over the last day, it struck me again, that there are so many things for which I am proud of Sam, but the most important to me is how he treated people. Sam never looked at someone and said, "I'm smarter than him," or "that kid is on the spectrum," or "that old lady is weird and smells funny." He saw everyone as equally important, interesting, wise in their own way, and most importantly, worthy of love. The only people he didn't like (there are three of them in his entire life; one he tolerated) were people who treated others as lesser beings and were snotty to those who are more vulnerable. In the end, the encounter yesterday served as a reminder that I need to "re-up" my following of Sam's lead in this, and for that, I give thanks for the jerk we met yesterday. The quote we have used to describe Sam's love is, "The greatest gift that you can give to others is the gift of unconditional love and acceptance." What better gift can we give others?

and

There are no words to describe how touched we are, or how irritatingly proud Sam would be with this news. He loved you all, was so happy that Z. had found such an amazing woman with whom to share his life. We send our love, thanks, and can't wait to meet Samuel—he will have to hear the story about his Daddy and Sam taking the sheep places.

The news? Sam's friend Z and his love were having their second child, a boy, and his name would be Samuel. I could hear Linnea's voice telling me Sam wanted a little army of Sams. I cried when I heard the news, out of sheer love.

Tuesday, December 16, 2014

Today I read an article about how when you lose a child to overdose, you don't get the community response/support than if your child had been killed in an accident or something more palatable to the community. We, as a family, overall felt community support as Sam's issues became publicly known, probably mostly because even in that darkness, the beauty and light of his soul shone through. But even in his death, there were people who said my mom should not have mentioned that drugs killed him at his service, that we could have said he died of something else. We have felt overwhelming support of our local community and our FB friends since his death, but we also know that many, many families don't have that support. We still, as a country, make negative comments about the mentally ill and addicts, dismissing them as less than human, as losers, as weak. Please, think about the families you know who walk through this valley of hell every single day, live in constant fear of the safety of their children, and stay awake at night racking their brains as to what they did wrong to "make" their children have these issues, and think how any act of kindness could help make their lives a little less hopeless. And to all of you who held our hands, brought soup, and have welcomed us into this discussion, thank you.

Wednesday, December 24, 2014

Tonight was a milestone for us as a family, as it is my dad's last Christmas Eve service—he retires this coming Sunday. With just a couple years of exception when he stepped away from a church for a bit, I have spent every Christmas Eve at one of his services. As always, it was beautiful.

Thursday, December 25, 2014

We wish you all a Merry Christmas. Our day was full of love, laughter, memories of good times, new experiences (Sora playing with Ben's phone, for example), some tears, and incredible support from friends and family.

Saturday, December 27, 2014

For those of you going to Twiddle tonight or tomorrow night, Twiddle hard with love and joy, and feel Sam's soul there loving every moment of the experience!

Sunday, December 28, 2014

Congratulations to my dad on his retirement today. Except for a short time while I was in late high school/early college, he has been full time in a church for longer than my entire life—in fact his official ministry is 55 years long. While I fully admit to having a lot of issues with organized religion, and with God over the last year and a half, I still have the deepest respect and admiration for his ministry and for his example for me. I'm really not sure what the heck he will do now with his time, but it was a beautiful and deeply meaningful service today, and I am so glad that current and past parishioners could be there.

and

Sam, your baby brother will be twiddling tonight with Linnea and Will and others—make your presence known to all.

and

Lots and lots of emotions today—dad's retirement, Ben going to Twiddle, and Ryan heading out to play hockey wearing a lot of Sam's equipment. How hard Sam would have laughed at the hymn that had a polka chorus in it, how excited he would have been to be with Ben at Twiddle, and how much he would have loved to take to the ice with Ryan.

What a strange mix of emotions: joy, pride, and absolute grief. How much I wanted to have Sam there in person for each of those things, and the best I could do was know that his spirit would be there with them.

Wednesday, December 31, 2014

As 2014 draws to a close, there are so many moments/people to be thankful for—I promise I am not going to list them all out here. A few, Sora's birth and health, seeing Amie become such an amazing mom, seeing the amazing young man that Ben continues to be and become (and OV theater being picked to go to Scotland, and his being picked for HOBY), seeing Ryan come back home/find a great job/find peace in himself, seeing Thayer and Bill, Paul's happiness in his farming and working in the shop, my new job, spending more time with Pauline and her family, getting back into more consistent contact with Kristen and Krista, the constant support of Bamby and Cheryl, Jean making me laugh and kicking me in the behind when I need it, and Ed and his old pictures and his patience with my folks. Then there are the friends that Sam brought into our lives, who make us laugh, cry with us, keep his memory alive, and just provide support far beyond what we can express. Finally, I am thankful beyond words for Paul. I wish you all joy, love and peace in 2015!

Plants, Pictures, Opiates, and Pain

W e had started our second year without Sam. By now, the number of my posts were dwindling, partially because I wondered if I had worn out people's patience by posting each day.

Wednesday, January 14, 2015

This post has been a long time in the making, as I have wrestled with how to say what I wanted to say. This is not meant to offend anyone. I have to say that over the last month, many of my FB friends have posted complaints about their children; how the hardest thing they ever had to do was see their child go back to college, how tiring it is to be a parent, etc. I am not saying that any of those feelings aren't valid, but I would suggest gently that being tired because your children have been happily busy on that day, or even because they are being difficult—this is a GIFT to you, be thankful for their presence in your life, be thankful they are there to irritate you, be thankful that you are dropping them off at college instead of picking out a casket. To see people whine about a gift they have seems almost sin-like to me. I recognize that parenting is difficult, and believe me, there are times when my kids irritate the daylights out of me, but my "new" perspective makes it so those little irritations don't mean as much as they once did. Who cares about dirty dishes left in the sink? Who cares about the Legos left on the floor? Who cares about the little ding in the car door? None of these matter if you can hold that child close, hear his/her voice, smell his/her unique smell, feed them a favorite food. To my friends who post the joys of parenthood, or at least recognize the gifts they have—thank you, thank you, thank you.

Friday, January 16, 2015

So now I will say it. Yesterday I had major surgery. It was planned and anticipated, but then needed to be moved sooner. I didn't share that info here for two reasons. One, I didn't want to talk about it anymore than needed—ewww, gross. Two, I was so scared and emotionally wound about it that I (with few exceptions) couldn't let my protective "shield" down for that. But, it went well, and the surgical team was beyond amazing. It will be a lengthy recovery, but I am so glad to be in that phase now. I would ask that at least for the next week, if you are trying to reach me that you use email, texts, or FB messages, as I will be trying to sleep when I can, and ringing phones don't help. As of right now, we are set for meals (great having a chef in the house), and with taking care of the animals, house etc. I promise to post if there is something that we need. To those of you who have held my hand through the lead-up, helped me at work, answered my late-night meltdowns, nagged me to stay hydrated and eat enough spinach, thank you. To my grandma, thank you for teaching me to knit. To Jean, Nancy, Erika, and Debra, thank you for being my sounding board. To Kristen, thank you for being there through it all, making me laugh, and texting with me at midnight last night. To Ed, thanks for always keeping me grounded. To my parents and Paul's parents, thank you for your love, trips to the store, and worry. To Ben and Ryan, thank you for putting up with the tears, and for watching Mamma Mia *with me on Wednesday night. For Tess, thank you for your skills, and for being my hand-holding friend. To Sam, thanks for all the signs of your presence over the last couple days. To Pope Francis, thanks for the amazing timing on the very specific prayers posted. I also give thanks for earbuds and my iPod. And I give thanks for Paul, who has held my hand through tests, procedures, tears, pain, made meals, etc., and always with gentleness and humor—you know a man loves you when he offers to watch Dirty Dancing with you if it would help distract you! I hope to go home today—can't wait to look out the window at the chickens and alpacas. Love to you all!*

Thursday, February 5, 2015

Again, I admit that today it is difficult to see the wonders of the world, but these three plants helped a lot. The first, an orchid which is blooming again—it keeps going and going! The second, a geranium given to us by Vanessa on the anniversary of Sam's death — he loved geraniums so much, and this plant has brought us great joy, and suddenly it is going crazy with growth. The third, is one of Sam's hot pepper plants. This one was a runt, forgotten on the back deck all summer, but I couldn't just toss it out—it came inside for the fall/winter, and suddenly it has taken off, new leaves each day, and a baby blossom has formed. The beauty and symbolism of the three plants helps more than I can express.

Tuesday, February 10, 2015

Sam—no matter how you were struggling, you saw the beauty and wonder around you. Thank you for teaching me that, and for reminding me of it today.

Thursday, February 12, 2015

Truck day makes me realize it is almost spring, regardless of the snow and cold. Patty and Ben, Happy Truck Day!

and

To those of you going to Twiddle tonight, twiddle hard, with joy and love, and look for signs of Sam there.

Saturday, February 14, 2015

As it is Valentine's Day, I have thought a lot about love over the last days and really, months. Someone once wrote that great (size not good) grief comes from great love. So true. Then I've come to realize how many of you I have told I love over these last months and have meant it with every ounce of my heart and soul. One of the side effects of my cousin's death many years ago was that my family has consistently made an effort to tell each other that we love each other and say it often. It is the last thing said in phone conversations, as one of us goes out the door, last part of a text, etc. We mean it fully, and while we know the love is there, why not express it? As many of you know, the last words Sam said to me, Paul, Ben, Mormor and Beepa was that he loved us, and we said it too. I know that he often said it to many of you too. The comfort that comes in knowing that is huge. But, since Sam's death, we have also come to the point of saying there are so many of you that we love, and so what if people think we are odd? We are going to say it out loud. We love you, we are thankful for you, we love having you in our lives. On this Valentine's Day, I am thankful for the romantic love I share with Paul, as well as his being my best friend. I am also thankful for the love of my family and friends, who don't just wait for February 14th to show their feelings—thank you to you all! And to all of you, I hope today (and every day) is filled with love and joy.

Sunday, February 22, 2015

As some of you know, the last few days have been a storm of grief for us—don't know what really set it off, but it has been truly difficult. There have been some irritating moments that disheartened us (like the creep Paul encountered on Friday) or when vehicles were getting stuck like crazy. But, then there were moments of kindness and beauty and love and laughter. Thank you to you all for your part in making this journey more bearable.

Wednesday, February 25, 2015

Some days, how my brain works makes me laugh. Today, I am trying to sort through a very small box of Sam's "stuff." I went into the project with the idea that I just have to get through it—no way around it, just go through it. That led me to suddenly hear the song "Mud" in my head. For those of you who spent any time with Sam at Leicester School, you know that Sam liked to sing LOUDLY. He sang all of Mormor's songs at LCS at the top of his voice, including "Mud." One of the lines is, "I can't go around it, I've gotta go through it." So, I guess the moral of the story today is, that I can't go around this box any more, I've got to go through it, with all of the associated emotions—but, I can sing the song loudly while I do it, and I will smile as I think about that stupid song and him singing it with his LCS family. Besides, as his beloved Arlo Guthrie would say (and he would quote in his perfect imitation), "If you want to end war and stuff you got to sing loud."

Friday, February 27, 2015

Yesterday, as I continued going through the little box of Sam's stuff, I opened his treasure box that had the label on it saying, "Sam's treasure box, do NOT ever open." So, when I opened it, the picture of Lake Dunmore that Sam had taken years and years ago was sitting on the very top. It took my breath away, because, as some of you know, when I was designing a tattoo to remind me why I need to keep getting up putting one foot in front of the other, I had a dream of Sam reminding me of how much he loved the green hills and silver waters of Vermont—so I took the image of Rattlesnake Point mountain from the beach at Branbury and put it in the tattoo. To open the box and find that he had taken and kept that picture was a gift beyond what I can express.

I almost didn't open that box. We have always taught our children that unless safety is involved, we will always respect their privacy. But that label intrigued me. What had Sam wanted to protect so badly? Slowly, I opened it and saw the picture. That picture had the *exact* same vantage point that I had used for the tattoo. The exact one. When Sam sent me that message of what to put in the tattoo, he clearly led me to the spot I chose, and to find that picture gave me great peace in knowing I'd chosen correctly.

___

Sunday, March 1, 2015

This weekend was full of Otter Valley Walking Stick Theater pro-ductions—as always, the One Acts were exceedingly well done. It is bittersweet to be there, the joy and excitement of seeing Ben and his friends perform, and the sadness of Sam not being there in body to cheer and give commentary. Over the course of the weekend, there were so many people who brought joy and support to us—thank you.

___

Sunday, March 8, 2015

This has been a farming-type weekend, for which I am very thankful. Yesterday, Paul and I tapped trees, something we had talked about for more than 20 years, then we planted the rest of our seedlings for the garden. Today, we transplanted more than 60 tomato plants and a bunch of calendula plants, thinned other seedlings, checked buckets, watched two parades of deer, then kept seeing the flock of turkeys. Now a pot of soup from one of our chickens, made with our beet greens, celery leaves, dried kale, garlic and onions is simmer-ing on the stove. This sort of weekend does our souls a lot of good!

___

Wednesday, April 8, 2015

Today, the 18-month mark, hit me harder than I can say. There are not enough words to express how much I miss Sam, but, this morning as I drove to work, this rainbow appeared in the clouds. It lifted my spirits and reminded me that little signs of his presence are around us.

___

Monday, April 13, 2015

As we have been on this journey of grief, it has irritated me when well-meaning people have made comments such as, "he's in a better place," or "he'll be forever young." I understand the good intentions, but I think the best possible place for Sam was/is being alive and with

his family and friends, and I never wanted him to be forever young—I
wanted to watch him grow old, achieve all his dreams (even the really
crazy ones), and to have so many more hours and days and weeks and
months, and preferably, years with him. So, as I was putting away a
suit coat yesterday, I found this in the pocket—Sam was the last person
to wear the jacket, and I have to say, it made me smile to see this ticket.

The "this"? It was a prom ticket tucked into his suit coat, and the theme of
the prom was "Forever Young." I couldn't decide whether to laugh or cry, so
I ended up sitting on the floor, surrounded by piles of stuff, and laughed while
tears streamed down my cheeks.

Thursday, May 7, 2015

Yesterday besides the joy of celebrating Ben's birthday, we also
celebrated an important anniversary for us. It was four years ago
yesterday that Sam brought Linnea home to meet all of us for the
first time—Francoeur/Holsman family events are not for the faint
of heart, but she survived it and even came back again. There are
no words to express our thankfulness for Sam bringing her into our
lives, or to express how important she is to all of us.

Friday, May 8, 2015

After work today, we really needed to go grocery shopping—not
even the "good" backup dinner options were left. I really, really
wanted to forget about it tonight and wait until tomorrow, but
tomorrow is very full, so I knew that wasn't an option. Luckily, we
went shopping, because we got to see Michaela and Jon, both of
whom made us smile and laugh, and reminded of us of the amazing
people we have in our lives because Sam brought them. So glad we
went grocery shopping after all!

Sunday, May 10, 2015

Happy Mothers' Day to all of the mothers out there—may your day
be filled with love and joy. I am so thankful for my mother, who

taught me how to be independent, loving and strong, and for my daughter who is one heck of a mom. And I am so thankful to my four children for making me a mom. A special Happy Mothers' Day to all of the step-moms out there, who aren't really sure where they fit today, but raised children with love and devotion, even when much of popular culture made the term stepmother sound evil. And finally, Happy Mothers' Day to my fellow "angel moms." Thank you for your love and support and guidance and patience. May your day be filled with love and great memories.

Friday, May 15, 2015

To all of our amazing young friends, brought into our lives by Sam, who will be graduating from college this weekend (or next, or did last weekend, etc.)—we wish you joy, love, success, happiness and the knowledge that you are absolutely amazing!

I really wanted to celebrate for those kids, I did. But I couldn't really do it, at least not well. I wanted to have Sam around, graduating or not, and all of the hoopla of his friends graduating ripped my heart into shreds no matter how much I love them, no matter how much I was happy for them.

Thursday, June 4, 2015

Otter Valley's show in the Fringe Festival is listed in their catalog!

Each day, we planned and prepared for our trip to Scotland. We kept holding onto the excitement of the trip, feeling like it would break us out of our negative rut.

Sunday, June 7, 2015

It has been almost a month since I last posted much of anything about things/people that make me thankful. As I have said before, this is not because I don't generally find something to be thankful for, but between being really busy, and struggling with grief, it can be difficult to see things clearly. So, belatedly, here it is. I am thankful to my chickens and alpacas, who make me laugh, give us food and fiber, and help keep us grounded. I am thankful to "Lucky" the meat chicken who instead gets to be a layer because we were able to heal her bad legs, and she is now part of the family. I am thankful for Sam's garlic garden, and for his tree, both of which are growing like crazy, and give me a small measure of peace. I am thankful for all the wonderful things Ben does, and for him receiving public recognition of them—he deserves it. I am thankful for seeing Ryan find his peace and seeing him find activities that bring him joy. I am thankful for Sora who reminds us that everything happens in its own time. I am thankful for seeing what a wonderful teacher Amie is, and how proud we are of her new job for next year. I am thankful for going to a retirement party last week for Glenn, one of the two best professors I ever had, and an amazing person. Honoring him was great, as was seeing so many people from my childhood. I am thankful that my cousin is happy with his new business venture. I am thankful for the wonderful Otter Valley community, and for Ray and his devotion to helping us keep Sam's legacy alive. I am thankful to Linnea and Leah for being part of our journey and being just plain fun to be around. I am thankful for spinning, knitting and cooking, all of which help slow my brain down. I am thankful for Cody, who helps remind me that grace and dignity are not determined by age—he and Carter are amazing. I am thankful for my parents, who as we adjust to our new selves in our new-ish reality, they are still always there. I am thankful to the other parents who are part of this lousy club with us, who are never too busy to hold out their arms in a literal or figurative hug. Wishing you all a joy and love-filled day.

Thursday, June 18, 2015

Tonight, our hearts are broken with those of the nation as we look to Charleston and are also broken for the family who lost two sons in Burlington, Vermont due to an apparent overdose.

Each day, more and more news stories reported the growing toll of opiate addiction across the country. Vermont had made the news in 2014 when *Rolling Stone* magazine had a cover story about the heroin issue. The trouble was that we were hearing more and more about heroin, but almost nothing about prescription overdoses. No one wanted to recognize the issues growing from the overprescribing of medications leading to addiction, leading to theft, leading to death in so many cases. Seeing the story on the local news that a family lost two sons in less than twenty-four hours to overdoses? It broke my heart again. How could their parents survive that? I wrote these complete strangers a note, expressing my sorrow. I don't know if it meant anything to them, but it helped me feel that I had recognized those lives.

Every day there were increasing numbers of posts online about the opiate issues. People made comments about how drug users were weak, that they didn't deserve anything other than incarceration, or worse. I read posts by people I respect, making comments about addicts and how they were less than human, and I felt so lost and hurt, so unsure of what to do. How could people who were so supportive of us in person write about how it was wrong to provide Narcan?

Trying to find something positive, something to break the routine, we decided to take a trip to Montreal with Ben and a friend. The women's World Cup was playing there, and we wanted to see a game. After two days in Montreal, wandering the underground city, visiting McGill University, and loving every minute of the game, we came home where I posted three pictures and the following words:

Saturday, June 27, 2015

Last night we were fortunate to see the France/Germany Women's FIFA game—great game, great venue, and lots of fun! Still wish France had won! Second picture (very blurry), when we got home, a doe with her tiny fawn. Third picture, in case there was any doubt that we are weird, we are growing Shiitake mushrooms.

For a couple of days, I seemed to feel a bit better/lighter overall. Then July came, and I found myself starting to slide again.

Friday, July 3, 2015

Over the past weeks, I have been trying to keep going forward, although with summer comes the wonderful and painful memories.

As some of you know, most of the time, I can go through the day pretty well, but come around 4 p.m., on my way home from work, it hits like a freight train as Sam would always call me on my way home to see how my day had gone and to find out what was on the dinner menu. Some days I force myself to not fall apart, sometimes I give in, and sometimes I need to "kick the bucket over" so the pressure dissipates. Yesterday afternoon was a bucket kicking time, and so I was listening to "Hattibagan McRat" by Twiddle, singing along, knowing full well that when I get to the line "and then I knew he was helping angels find their feet," that I would cry for a bit. That line came on about 10 feet before my driveway, and when I stopped to get the mail, there was a piece of mail addressed to "Sam Frankcoeur" from the Flock Dance Troupe (thanks to Allie for introducing Sam to them), with the quote on it that said, "I don't care how many angels can dance on the head of a pin. It's enough to know that for some people they exist, and that they can dance. (Mary Oliver)" One of the things I have come to accept over these last months is that there are things that I don't fully understand, but that "forces" are at work—reading that quote made me laugh and gave me comfort and a moment of peace.

Thursday, July 9, 2015

Emotional tirade alert—I have to admit to a level of frustration with the huge uptick in media coverage of the heroin problem in the United States. I totally agree that heroin is a huge problem, but as the media focuses on that topic, they are missing a MUCH larger issue. The NIH reports that in 2013, 22,500 people died of prescription drug overdoses (Sam being one), while 8500 people died of heroin overdoses. Again, my heart breaks for any family who has lost someone to any kind of overdose, but the scope of the prescription drug issue is mind-blowing and is being ignored for the most part. Is it because it's easier to focus our attention on illegal drugs? Is it because of the big money involved in the legal pharmaceutical world? Again, not saying we shouldn't look at the heroin issue, but why not give the prescription issue as much attention?

Friday, July 24, 2015

Sam, as I promised you we would be, we will be going to see Arlo Guthrie perform Alice's Restaurant *in October.*

As I found myself getting more and more wound about Sam's coming birthday, suddenly the Alice's Restaurant tour announced the Rutland date and the tickets sent on sale. With a lump in my throat, we ordered the tickets, knowing that we needed to go to that concert.

Thursday, July 30, 2015

Happy 22nd birthday (forever 20) to Sam we love you and miss you more than we can express, and I hope that today you are having cheeseburgers, Annie's, cucumbers and trifle. We will be farming in your honor today and will then spend time outside in some of your other favorite places.

and

If anyone sees a rainbow today, please take a picture and post it.

Friday, July 31, 2015

Thank you to all of our friends and family for the incredible support every day, but especially this week. For both Paul and I, Sam's birthday yesterday hit us much harder than we expected. July 30 will always be the anniversary of one of the most joyous days of our lives but will forever bring sadness too without Sam being here in person to celebrate his special day. But, virtual and in-person hugs, texts, emails, posts on Sam's page, visits, and just knowing how many of you out there support us, and miss him, makes it more bearable.

Scotland, A Volcano, and Sam's Roslyn Rainbow

With August came the excitement of our upcoming trip to Scotland, as well as the bone-chilling fear of Ben traveling to England, then Scotland, without us. At the end of the first week of August, Otter Valley gave a public performance of *Anonymous*, the play they would perform in the Fringe Festival—and Ben starred as Anon. On that night, we were so thrilled to have our friend Leah join us, as she said, representing Linnea.

Saturday, August 8, 2015

The play at Otter Valley was amazing last night! What an amazing job the thespians did, and we are so glad we get to see them perform it again in Scotland. It was especially wonderful to have Leah join us to watch it!

Two days later, Ben got on a tour bus with the group, and headed out. Watching him get on that bus was both so exciting and so terrifying. We drove away, telling ourselves it would all be fine, and that we would be back together with him soon. The plan was simple: the theater group was flying to London, spending a couple of days in England before taking the train to Scotland. We were leaving the next day, and going directly to Scotland, planning to meet him in Edinburgh.

We got to Scotland after having the best travel experience of our lives. No one has ever had travel go that smoothly! Flights were on time, we had a whole row to ourselves, and the flight crew was relaxed and friendly. They even gave us extra food and beverages because so few people were on the flight. At the Edinburgh airport, we sailed through immigration. Then, in a first for us, we got on a city bus (instead of taking a taxi) and rode to meet the owner of the apartment we were renting for our stay.

At his shop, our landlord welcomed us like family. We had only communicated with him via one phone call and emails, but when we met in person, it was like we'd known each other forever. With a smile, he told us that the apartment was still being cleaned, so if we wanted to wander the neighborhood around his shop for a bit, he would then drive us over and get us settled. Here we were expecting that once we got the key, we'd take a taxi, and instead, he said he'd take us to make sure we were all set.

Slightly punchy from lack of sleep and being in a completely different time zone, we wandered through a fabulous craft fair, looking at art from local vendors. We had a snack and sat in the sunshine, laughing about the sign for "bangers and mash," which Sam had eaten with such gusto when we'd gone to London (and Legoland) as a family.

A few hours later, we walked back to his shop and our landlord took us on a driving tour of the city and got us settled in our new temporary home. The apartment was in a perfect location, and was a hoot. Zebra print pillows graced the bed, the living room chairs had animal print, and we had three, count them, three electric tea pots. It was a great place, and so different that it truly felt like we were a world apart. We took about a hundred pictures of the place, sending them to Linnea and Ryan, and couldn't wait to have Ben see it when he got to Scotland.

Then we slept. Frankly, I think it was the first night since Sam had died that the two of us slept through the entire night; in fact, we didn't wake up until almost noon the next day. Finally awake, we stocked up on groceries, walked around the neighborhood, and went back to make a real meal in our lovely little kitchen as we listened to the local radio.

Saturday, August 15, 2015

Listening to the radio in Edinburgh, and they played "Sweet Caro-line," and then the announcer said that he felt everyone needed to go to a baseball game in the U.S. to see the Americans sing along— that it was a wonderful experience! Made me remember a time when Ben's all-star team sang it in the dugout during a game delay.

———————

Hearing "Sweet Caroline" made us smile as we remembered a family memory that we could just plain enjoy, no weight of grief to pull us down. With a smile, we posted that online, and several of the baseball parents imme-diately responded, making us smile even more.

After dinner that night, we walked through the royal garden/estate, around the base of Arthur's Seat—an extinct volcano—to the University of Edin-burgh to see Ben for just a few minutes. We needed to walk almost three miles to get to the university to put eyes on him, wanting to see him in person instead of just messaging him. Sitting with him on the bench outside his dorm, looking at the luscious flowers, we chatted about his trip, including all the travel challenges they'd encountered, and laughed about how easy our trip had been.

Over the next two weeks, we talked about how gorgeous Scotland was. Green, lush, harsh, wild. We loved wandering the countryside or walking through the city. And Ben's play? What a thrill to see your child perform in an international venue and do it so well.

While we were there, we agreed to help out at the shows. The school needed to provide a fire marshal for each performance, so we were officially trained to serve in that role for their shows. Just before their last performance, we were standing by the door to the theater, waiting to take our official seat once the door was ready to be closed, and a man came running up the stairs, shouting, "Is this Anon?" in this thick brogue. We nodded, shocked into silence. This young man had more piercings than anyone I'd ever seen, every inch of visible skin other than his face was covered in intricate tattoos, and frankly he was rather imposing. In a dark alley, he'd have been terrifying. Long hair, bandanna, leather jacket, the works. In our minds, we kept won-dering what the heck he was doing at that performance.

At the end of the show, that man stood up, clapping and cheering. He then strode over to us, and asked about one of the other actors in Ben's group. Why did he want to see him? What was the connection? All of a sudden, the named actor came out, saw this stranger, and ran toward him. Ran. And they hugged and hugged. I know our mouths hung open in shock. This stranger was there to see the recipient of Sam's scholarship; he'd met the other actor years before at summer camp, and came to see him perform. After meeting him, and having a lovely conversation, Paul and I walked back to the bus stop talking about how that was a perfect Sam moment. Sam would have loved that guy…

One of the other benefits to the entire trip was learning more about people we had known for years, namely the two directors for OV's theater program. We'd known them, but in Scotland, we got to know each other in a whole new way. We found out about their other interests, their sense of humor, and how they handled stress and a huge group of crazy and temperamental actors in a foreign country.

Friday, August 21, 2015

Will and Sam, yesterday we went by the castle used in the Holy Grail—made me laugh to think of you doing your "bits" from it.

On that Friday, we went to Loch Ness for Sam. Sam loved legends like that of Nessie, and every single time we crossed Lake Champlain, he'd searched for Champ, our local lake monster. When Ben had announced he was going to Scotland, and then we decided to go, we made the decision that the three of us were going to Loch Ness for Sam. We spent such a wonderful day traveling through the countryside, Ben sleeping on Paul's shoulder, visiting villages, then going to Loch Ness and putting our toes in the water, laughing about great family trips, and talking about how much Sam would have loved that day.

Saturday, August 22, 2015

So, some of you know I have a huge fear of heights, but, successfully climbed Arthur's Seat yesterday with the guys.

On our next to the last full day in Scotland, we went gift shopping with Ben, which meant I somehow got stuck with a huge bag of scarves to carry around. Then we (finally) hiked Arthur's Seat, just the three of us, because after all, when you have an extinct volcano in the neighborhood, you need to climb the thing.

I am terrified of heights. But Ben didn't know that, because I'd managed to keep it a secret from the kids their entire lives. We were going to climb that volcano and there was no way on this Earth that I was going to not go, so I swallowed my terror and climbed. I did okay going up, loved taking a picture at the top, then held Paul's hand in a death grip going down because I could see how far we had really climbed. I don't often think of the word "proud" about things I have done, but I was, and am, proud of climbing that volcano.

On our last day in Scotland, we went to Rosalyn Chapel. We had planned to go, but then canceled our plans, feeling we needed a breather before the trip home—especially since we were getting back late in the afternoon and school was starting the next morning. But our landlord kept calling us and telling us we needed to go there, really kind of pushing us to go. So we did. And we are so thankful we went—great village, beautiful chapel, incredible history, delicious pastries, lots of laughs as we remembered how much Sam had been interested in the legends of the Knights Templar. Then we asked another tourist to take a photo of us, and as we flew home and looked at the photos, there was a rainbow almost showering down on us on this perfectly clear day. Sam had approved of us going there.

CHAPTER TWENTY-SIX

Stigma, Soccer, Arlo, an Anniversary, and Holidays

Now we were home, after a wonderful two weeks in Scotland, thrust immediately into the school year, and more importantly, into Ben's senior year. While we had so enjoyed our trip, after planning it for over a year, the letdown of it being over was crushing. So we jumped into Ben's soccer season, finished up the gardening harvest, and looked for the positives, all the while pretending we weren't dreading October.

Saturday, September 12, 2015

Two tirades this morning, unfortunately related— first, I am appalled that yesterday on "Fresh Air" Terry Gross said, "How does a 17-year-old like you, who is deeply into literature and music and really smart... end up doing heroin? ... Smart enough to know how dangerous it is." That someone educated would make such an ignorant and public comment is heartbreaking—I guess only stupid, non-readers are supposed to get addicted. Too bad Sam didn't know that... Second tirade, I wish the media would stop referring to Biden as "still mourning." He will mourn for the rest of his life, so I wish they would stop making it sound like he should snap out of it. As cranky as those tirades sound, before you amazing people worry

about my state of mind today, I'm okay, actually doing pretty well,
but just needed to say both of them out loud. Love to you all!

As I kept seeing and hearing comments about addiction, comments about drug users, I kept struggling with the ignorance; it has been a struggle my entire life. When I was in eighth grade, I finally worked up the nerve to go in to my school guidance counselor to tell her that my father was an alcoholic and that I needed help. Her response: "Your father is a minister and on the school board. He can't be an alcoholic." When she said that, I learned that I needed to keep it a secret, which I did for several more years.

Sunday, September 13, 2015

What did we do so far today? We picked in the garden, froze 3 huge
heads of cabbage, froze packages of plum tomatoes, canned 7 pints
of dilly beans and 12 pints of pickled swiss chard/kale, made lac-
to-fermented beets and turnips, have a huge pan of root vegetables
roasting, made gallons of vegetable stock from the trimmings from
canning, roasted one of the meat chickens we raised this year, made
a huge pot of mac-n-cheese, then made several loaves of pumpkin
bread—love being mostly self-sufficient in our food growth and pro-
duction/love being a locavore otherwise!

Being a locavore and enjoying the things we grew helped immensely. I tried not to be obnoxious about how often I posted about these things, but they mattered so much to me that I needed to share.

Saturday, September 26, 2015

While it is highly unlikely that I will ever become a Catholic, I admire
Pope Francis greatly—and reading his words from 2013 to patients
in an addiction recovery program makes me admire him even more!

At the beginning of October, we had three milestones looming. First, on October 6th, Paul, Ben, my parents, and I would go to see Arlo Guthrie perform *Alice's Restaurant*, keeping our promise to Sam.

Wednesday, October 7, 2015

How thankful I am for having the opportunity to go see Arlo Guth-
rie and his band last night at the Paramount Theater in Rutland
with Paul, Ben, my mom and dad, and then getting to see Mitch
and Maureen, and Hannah and John—to be there to see such great
music, and to feel the amazing emotion of doing something we had
promised Sam we would do, was quite a ride!

———

I admit that I was anxious going to that concert. Right before, we'd gone for pizza, then went to meet my parents at the theater. Walking into the theater where we had seen so many performances, including seeing Arlo there with Sam, I could feel myself choke up. Sitting down, we made small talk for a bit, before we realized that Will's parents were sitting right near by, then Allie's mom came to see us. By the time the lights dimmed, I was more in the zone of feeling the love than feeling the loss.

The concert was amazing. Every moment of it was just as it should have been. We laughed, we cried and we sang along. Going home that night, I felt joy and peace that we'd gone.

That week we also had Ben's senior soccer game, which is a big deal at Otter Valley. Seniors are honored, parents are recognized, and even under "normal" circumstances, it's really emotional. To have Ben's senior game on October 8th was a bit much emotionally; we were already so raw, but it was a beautiful day full of love, joy, tears, laughter, including Garrett screaming, "I love you, Ben," at the top of his lungs, making Ben grin from ear to ear.

Then we had "the anniversary." And for the first time (okay, it was only the second anniversary), I didn't post on the day itself.

———

Sunday, October 11, 2015

Yesterday morning, Facebook popped up a memory—a post from
October 10, 2013, when I let our FB friends and family know that
Sam had passed away. Opening FB first thing in the morning and
seeing this photo, still one of my all-time favorites of Sam (thanks
Allie!) took my breath away I didn't need FB to tell me what this
weekend is in terms of date/significance. So, here is what I figured out

over the last week about our path. First, I went into this past week full of dread and anticipation. Going to see Arlo do "Alice's Restaurant" has always been a dream of mine, one I shared with Sam. Going to the Paramount, remembering how much fun we had the last time we went there together, was both beautiful and painful. It was an amazing show, and in the end, I felt more joy and peace than I expected. Then, we had Ben's senior soccer game, falling exactly 2 years to the day that we last saw Sam alive on those bleachers, at a game as he often was to cheer on his baby brother. The anticipated emotion of it being Ben's senior game, and not having Sam there in person scared me—but at the end of the day, we talked about how that afternoon had nothing but beauty, joy and love in it. Thanks to Bernadette, Garrett and Haley, and Muffie for making the trip to join us for the game. Garrett and Muffie made all the joyful noise for Ben that Sam would have and brought laughter and joy to us. Then we had the 2nd anniversary. We had the day planned fully, deep down afraid of "down time." The rain completely messed up the plans, and instead we had a lot of down time, but it gave Paul and I the chance to talk a lot about our journey. Then, we had visitors, calls, emails and FB posts from friends and family, that reminded us of what an amazing community of support we have—people who reached out just to check on us all, to say Sam's name out loud, and to tell us how they continue to love and miss him. We laughed, we teared up, and we realized anew how lucky we are to have such great people in our lives.

Wednesday, October 21, 2015

Tonight was the last Varsity Boys' Soccer game of the season for OV, and therefore, Ben's last game at OV. Without hesitation, I can say that I have never seen a team act with such class and caring for each other and their opponents game after game, year after year. They have shown such class, such maturity, and am so thankful to have been able to watch this group of seniors in particular over these past years!

After that game, I just seemed to sort of hunker down, not posting directly, just doing some reposting of inspirational quotes. Finally, at the end of November, I posted:

Sunday, November 29, 2015

I thought a lot about posting as this long weekend comes to an end. As I hope you know, I try to be aware of being thankful, and most days, I think I do an okay job with it. Thanksgiving, however, as a holiday, hits me harder than I can express, mostly because Sam liked Thanksgiving more than any other holiday—you know, bring lots of people together, eat anything you want and lots of it, and show people how much you love them—it was his favorite. Then, add in always listening to "Alice's Restaurant", and you had a joy-filled holiday with him. To have him missing in person still hits like a freight train around any holiday or family event, but especially this one. Add to it missing friends who are too far away, and hearing of friends losing loved ones, and it was a bittersweet time. Having said that, it was a long weekend filled with so many wonderful moments for which I am so grateful. Gardening in t-shirts on Black Friday, opening new garden beds, putting the rest of the garden to bed for the winter, sitting by the fireplace with Paul, knowing that our cousin in Texas is doing so much better, talking with friends and family, getting to spend some time just hanging out with Ben and Ryan, watching Paul shell dried beans, knitting gifts, cooking really good food, taking lots of walks, and watching the chickens and the alpacas, all made me so thankful and brought peace and a measure of joy. To you all, thank you for your constant love, support, patience—it means so much, and I am so grateful to have you all as part of my life.

Monday, December 7, 2015

Sometimes something happens that makes you sad, even though it doesn't seem like a big deal in a global sense—Bove's Restaurant closing is one of those things. Our first date was there, and we have spent many afternoons/evenings there over the years for great meals, love and laughter.

On December 7th, there was a little story on the local news that a restaurant in Burlington was closing. No big deal, right? Wrong. I sat and cried. We had gone there on our first date, taken the kids there to celebrate milestones including when Ben and Sam had decided to go to UVM, and gone to dinner there on date nights. This was our "family" restaurant, and with it going, it again felt like bits of our past with Sam were being erased.

Then Linnea called, telling me that I needed to listen to Twiddle's new album, specifically to the song "White Light."

Saturday, December 12, 2015

("White Light") I've thought about this song a lot this week (thanks to Linnea) and come to the conclusion that Sam had internalized the idea of loving relentlessly—and in moments lately when people are irritating me, I try to hold to that idea. Deep down, I think we all need to listen to this song, read the lyrics and, more than anything, to love relentlessly.

Friday, December 25, 2015

Many of you know that for all the years my dad was minister in Hancock, we would stop at the top of the Ripton mountain after the service on Christmas Eve to leave a lit candle to bring light into the darkness—it wasn't our idea, we saw it one year as we went over the mountain and liked it so much that we adopted it as a family tradition. Year in and year out, we stopped. The last two Christmases before this one, we did it in Sam's honor—he loved to put the candle there, and then would have to listen to Pavarotti's "Ave Maria" really loudly. Last night, since dad has retired, we didn't go over the mountain, and instead put a bunch of candles around Sam's tree on the front lawn and listened to "Ave Maria" there. Christmas morning came, and the candles were still burning brightly—and tonight, one still burns.

and

To all of our friends and family, we send wishes of love and joy and peace to you all—thank you for being part of our lives!

Thursday, December 31, 2015

As 2015 comes to a close, I can't say that it has been an easy year—chronic health issues and grief have made it difficult. But, throughout, there have been moments of great joy, constant love and support, adventures, and throughout them all, signs of never-ending love. We give thanks for all of our friends and family—all of you bring us joy, show us how much you love us, and keep us going. Thank you all for all you do for/with us— it means more than you can know. As I look back on 2015, I am so very proud of Ben for his taking on the role in Anonymous, and for being so amazing in it in Scotland—that is a memory that I will treasure forever. From that trip, my "best" moment was the three of us climbing the volcano, so that is my photo of the year. To all of you, I wish you a 2016 filled with love and joy!

CHAPTER TWENTY-SEVEN

Love, Fluffy, the Play Inevitable, and Our First Twiddle Concert

2016 arrived with snow and ice everywhere, and I began to recognize some things I hadn't thought of before. First, I began to realize that we as a family had the obligation to do what we could for other families in similar situations, and we had the obligation to carry on Sam's legacy of love and acceptance. I also began to realize that no matter how much I loved my current job, I needed to make a professional change because the daily weight of the drive home and the daily reminder when I drove over that one particular hill that Sam was never going to call me again sunk in, and I also realized that having worked in the same school for sixteen years, my colleagues (as incredibly supportive as they were and are) struggled with how different I was now than the way I'd been pre-October 9, 2013. It wasn't their fault that my life had irrevocably changed, and I realized that as Ben's high school career came to an end, it was time for me to make a change too. So, with the full blessing and support of my supervisor, I started looking for opportunities that didn't have the same emotional weight. With all of this rolling around in my head, and my sneaking suspicion that people were sick of my online posts of gratitude, I began to post less and less, while still actively and consistently looking for reasons to be grateful each and every day, even if it didn't get mentioned on Facebook.

Sunday, January 10, 2016

In a weekend that has been difficult, we are so thankful for seeing people today who remind us of our blessings, thank you to those who are always there—and are never too busy to answer a text or an odd message. And finally, we are so thankful for the beautiful, beautiful rainbow that filled our sky this afternoon!

——— ——

Saturday, January 16, 2016

One of the things we have said over and over is that Sam brought the most amazing people into our lives! Yesterday, in a day when sadness was heavier than normal, we got a reminder of how he made sure that we would always have those amazing people around. To Will and Linnea, thank you for always being there, for always taking the time to be part of all of our lives, for remembering him with us with joy and laughter and sometimes some tears, and for helping us feel he is not forgotten. To their parents, you raised the most amazing kids—thank you for sharing them with us!

——— ——

After that post, I went into a strange period of introspection. I kept meaning to post during this time, and I did post a little, but almost exclusively birthday wishes, reposting of quotes that mattered to me, things like that. It was a combination of trying to wrestle with the idea that our "baby" was finishing high school, and that was a huge emotional weight for me, then the logistics of his college search/application process, and that I was also struggling with the reality that I really needed/wanted to look for a new job.

I did post a couple times about little things that made me smile: the gift of a CD of Will's singing group, Ben winning a local public speaking competition, a few small updates about our lives. In looking back at those few months, really, I think I was settling in to accept that Sam was really gone, not coming back. I thought that maybe people were tired of me posting my thanks so often. It was a dark time (but not overly so); more like a deep twilight for me, and it took a while for the dawn to again appear.

My first return to actively thinking about conscious thanks came with this relatively short post, exactly three months after my last real gratitude post:

——— ——

Tuesday, April 19, 2016

And finally, FB reminded me that five years ago, Fluffy came to live with us—she still thinks she's a cat or dog (loves to be carried, comes over to have her back rubbed, and talks when you speak to her), still faithfully lays eggs, and makes us laugh daily. The day she arrived, I had no idea how much joy she would bring!

———————

Fluffy. I still keep a picture of her on my phone. After that post, I went outside to visit with her, bringing her a little bowl of watermelon chunks, and sat on the slightly muddy lawn and hand-fed her, talking to her as she made all sorts of happy sounds back. Now, more than a year after her death, I still miss her terribly.

Taking a step backward in the timeline, early in the spring of 2016, Ben came home and told us that the Otter Valley One Act play was going to be a movement piece. Going on the assumption that a lot of you don't live in the high school theater world, the One Acts are plays that are prepared by each high school in New England who wants to compete, performing at their own school, then performing at a regional event. Judges determine which plays then go on to compete at the state level where they are judged again, and the two winners from each New England state go to the New England Drama Festival. If you're into high school theater, this is a huge deal.

So, when Ben came home and told us about the play, we rolled our eyes (not proud that we did that, but yes, we rolled our eyes and took a couple of really deep breaths). A movement piece? Seriously? Then he further explained that not only was it a movement piece, they (the students) were writing it, and choreographing it (with help), and he was one of the leads. Oh, goody, we figured it was going to be incredibly esoteric. Yes, we knew because Jeff was directing it, it would be incredibly well done, but we figured it was going to be something that we would somewhat endure, not necessarily enjoy except for the chance to see our child perform.

Over the next six weeks, Ben told us almost nothing about the play, so when we went to the opening night, we went with the idea that we were supporting our child and the program. We didn't expect to enjoy it, or be inspired by it. We were so wrong! Of all the performances we'd seen over the years, this was the best show, period. When Ben came off the stage to see us, we told him right then that we were going home to book a hotel for the New England event in Connecticut, because they were going to win the state competition—and they did! [You can watch the performance online—let's see how closely you are reading. If you'd like to watch the performance, either Google "Inevitable by Otter Valley Walking Stick Theater" or send me a message via my author's webpage and I will send you the link.]

Anyway, this play, it was truly one of the greatest works of theater I've ever seen. It was a piece of pounding music, jarring dance showing the development of two young men from being little boys on the playground to eventually becoming lovers. One of them (not Ben's role) struggled with his sexuality, and also had a girlfriend, and without any dialogue, it showed the pain of his journey. In the final minutes of the play, that character attempted suicide but survived—and yes, even years later, I feel my heart swell as I think about the power of that play.

The amazing thing? We are talking Vermont here. Vermont legalized civil unions before any other state, but there is little to no real diversity here. So sitting watching this play for the first time, I felt fear for the reaction of the high school students in that auditorium. Would they recognize the beauty and power of this piece, or would they make fun of the cast, especially the two male leads?

The play ended, and the front row of the audience, almost the entire football team, surged to their feet, cheering, clapping, showing the most beautiful support. They recognized the importance of the piece, and more than that, they recognized the strength of the cast demonstrated in performing it.

The play advanced in the rankings, blowing away the competition. At each stage, the audience gave rousing standing ovations, and you could see so many people crying because it had touched them so deeply.

There was one moment of absolute levity in the whole process. After the regional competition, Ben's girlfriend was waiting with us for him to come out. He came out, sweaty, still in stage makeup, and hugged her. She hugged him tightly, then pulled back, "Is that Jacob's shirt?" (Jacob was his co-star.)

"Yes." Ben looked sheepish. "I forgot my shirt, so I borrowed his."

She laughed. "I figured... you smell really, really good."

Between the play, Ben's senior year events, and my job search, it was a busy spring, one where we tried to balance all of the expectations with who we now were, or who we were all now becoming.

In early May, I interviewed for my dream job. Outside the interview, waiting in my car, I could feel the signs of an anxiety attack coming. What the heck was I doing, thinking of making a professional change while still so new in my grief? Why would they want me? In desperation, I called one of my safe people. In a calm voice, she told me that I was made for this job, they would be lucky to have me, and that I needed to remember that I was a "warrior woman." In her strong voice, she reminded me that I had survived what no one should ever have to survive, so a job interview would be a walk in the park. Walking into that interview, I kept whispering "warrior woman" under my breath.

We waited for news on that job, making sure all was ready for Ben to go to college in the fall as I was closing out the school year. Then in mid-May, we went to Ben's final theater performance, after which I wrote:

———

Saturday, May 14, 2016

For the last 12 years, the theater directors at OV have been a constant part of our family life through their directing OVWST. Their love, support, expectations of excellence, and belief in Sam and Ben inspired them to great performances—and the love and support they have shown us all as a family in our loss has been appreciated beyond belief. Otter Valley is so very lucky to have them both artistically and as overall role models for students! Jeff and Anita—thank you!

———

Then, a few days later I wrote:

———

Thursday, May 19, 2016

Okay, now I can say it officially—and I am so very excited!

———

After months of looking for a new professional opportunity, I landed my dream job—the role of middle school principal in the town where I had gone to junior high, high school, and college. I hadn't totally believed I had the best chance, but I threw my hat into the arena and was thrilled beyond belief when they offered me the job. I have to admit, it was really fun seeing an article on the front page of the local newspaper announcing my new position.

Leaving my old job brought a wave of emotion. Sam had helped me move into my teaching classroom in that school, he'd helped me move into my offices as an administrator, and routinely stopped by the school to say hi over the years. Now I was leaving that place for a new adventure, but this was one that he would never be able to see (not from an Earthly vantage point anyway).

The spring rolled on, and with it came another huge milestone—Ben's high school graduation. Not only was it huge for him, but due to the age range of our kids, it also marked the end of a more-than-20-year era of there being a Francoeur kid at Otter Valley, and that milestone was a really emotional one for us all. There was the absolute joy of his graduation (and how well he had done in high school) and the absolute sadness that Sam wasn't there in person to be part of it. There was the pain of walking by Sam's theater award case as we walked into the school gym, and the joy of seeing how the OV teachers treated Ben. What a roller coaster of emotions!

Saturday, June 11, 2016

So, in what may embarrass the heck out of him, I need to post about this guy. Happy graduation today to Ben! There is no way to adequately express how proud we are of him. We would have been so proud of his accomplishments regardless, but when you look at them through the lens of the challenges during his 18 years, they are mind-boggling. He is smart, courageous, fair, loyal, funny, graceful, tenacious, and humble about everything except his sense of fashion. Happy, happy graduation—we love you, and can't wait to see what great things are coming next!

Just a few days later, Facebook kicked me in the stomach, reminding me of my post when Sam's grave had been desecrated. As I re-read my original post, the rage hit me again, but as I tried to refocus, I wrote:

Tuesday, June 21, 2016

In the way FB does, this memory popped up this morning. For a moment, it rattled me badly as it made me relive the anger and sadness of that day. Then, I instead realized how that horrible event led me to see anew the wonder and beauty in the people around us. To Gary, who probably won't see this post, we thank him more than we can express for the endless hours he spent cleaning the stone for us, free of charge, just because in his mind, it was the right thing to do. Then, as time has passed, "things" appear at the grave, little trinkets, flowers, produce, etc. All of them have significance for the people who leave them, and they know that the items also have significance to Sam and show something of their relationship—and all show their love. So, to all of the visitors who come and sit with Sam for a moment, and sometimes leave something there, thank you.

Then, because we now follow Twiddle's Facebook page and website, we saw that they were planning a big weekend music festival on the waterfront in Burlington. In a coincidence that none of us feel really was a coincidence, the festival (their first) would be held on Sam's birthday weekend, on his actual birthday. Of course it would! How else would the universe celebrate the anniversary of his birth, but with joy, music, and love?

Paul, Ben, Ryan and I talked it over and decided to-go to the festival together to celebrate his birthday.

Tuesday, July 19, 2016

So, who will be Twiddling on Sam's birthday, July 30th, in Burlington on the waterfront?

Friday, July 29, 2016

As we go into Sam's birthday weekend, we are holding on to great memories of love and laughter. If you get a chance, please post/ share a photo or a memory of Sam, or if you don't want to share it on FB, talk to a friend about him—keeping that joy, love and enthusiasm alive.

and

Quoting Twiddle: "When it's time to shut your eyes, inside there's light that gives me life, too blind to see, so pure, so free, the love you gave to those in need, well I'm here my friend, this love won't end I'll spread your word, no I won't turn back when times cut short and all that's left is your sweet love."

Saturday, July 30, 2016

Happy, happy 23rd birthday to Sam—we miss you more than we can say, but your birthday will always be a celebration of having you in our lives!

and

If you are twiddling, come find us!

and

If anyone sees a rainbow today, please take a picture and post it.

and

Only Sam could make a rainbow shine in the sky above Twiddle for almost 90 minutes, on a beautiful and sunny day... Thanks to Lyndsay, Emily, Will, Ryan and Ben for being with us there tonight, and thanks to Linnea for always being no more than a phone call away—and thanks to you all for your love and support today and every day!

Driving to Burlington to go to Twiddle's Tumble Down, I was nervous. It sounds silly, being nervous going to a concert, but this was *so* much more than a concert. Going to see Twiddle was something I wished so very much I had done *with* Sam, but now at least I was doing it. Walking through the gate, the first person I really saw was a man dressed in a suit of fabric with bright yellow bananas on it, then a young woman wearing a neon pink tutu. With a chuckle, I looked at Paul, who said, "Yup, this is Sam's world."

The concert was beautiful, fun, loud under a sunny cloudless sky. The crowd was happy, dancing, wandering, and visiting. Sam's friends found us, we hugged, laughed, talked—and listened to the music and sang along.

Who would have thought before *that* day that we'd be at a Twiddle show singing along?

Then one of Sam's friends took my hand. "Kris, turn around."

I turned around, looking out over Lake Champlain and there, shimmering in the clear blue sky was a rainbow—a gorgeous rainbow. Yup, I cried. The friend cried. Paul, Ben, Ryan, and Sam's other friends all teared up, and there were lots of hugs, and tons of pictures taken of the rainbow. I took a picture of it and texted it to Linnea, knowing she would understand the significance.

CHAPTER TWENTY-EIGHT

Sam's Rainbow and Relentless Love

That rainbow on July 30, 2016 was the start of me "getting it." The rainbow shimmered in that perfect sky for over ninety minutes. All sorts of people who had no connection to Sam took pictures of it, and one of the musicians even mentioned it from the stage. Two months later, a person with whom I work, who knew nothing of Twiddle being a part of our lives, mentioned the rainbow at the concert because a friend of hers was there and talked about it. That was how odd but powerful that rainbow was.

But for me, that concert, that rainbow, was when I finally began to feel the acceptance. Not that I am, or ever will be, over losing Sam. You don't ever get over losing a child. But in that moment, seeing that rainbow on his birthday at a concert of his favorite band, with many of the people he loved most around us celebrating his birthday, I felt the beginning of the understanding of how infinite love is, how it doesn't die when someone's heart stops, and that if you can find your way through the haze of pain, you can still see signs of that love and you can bring good out of your pain.

Looking back on that rainbow, I realize how that was also the moment when I clearly realized that our understanding of the phases of existence (life vs death) is very rudimentary. I can't explain through science why there was a rainbow that day. I can't explain why a year later when we were traveling to see Linnea in a show that there was another vibrant rainbow in the sky on a perfectly clear day, or why when I went to my first book signing as an author there was one, then two rainbows—again, on a clear day. I can't explain by science or technology why my iPhone will suddenly start playing one of Sam's favorite songs when it's been removed from my music library. I can't explain how people call, text, email from all over the world to give us "messages" from Sam, and how comfortable they feel sharing them.

Then, the big one: as an author of fiction, I had written novels, submitted them, had them rejected, and put them away repeatedly over the years. Sam would bug me about it, telling me that I needed to keep trying, and that one day, I would have an agent or get a publishing contract, and then we would all go out to dinner and order whatever we wanted (if you're a child from a big family with financial constraints, you understand how big a deal ordering "whatever you want" is!). He'd tell me this with his huge smile, give me a hug, and tell me to keep trying.

After his death, I put aside my creative writing for a long, long time, but eventually, I decided I needed to honor his belief in me. I printed my two completed novels out, hired a great editor, and then started submitting them again, and in June of 2017, I was offered and signed my first publishing contract. Fast forward to October 2017, and my expected release date of my first novel, *That One Small Omission*, was set for October 11th. I had specifically picked the date for mid-October to give us a joyful new October anniversary and wanted to keep it separate from the emotions of each ninth of October.

Late on the night of October 9th, after having done my best to navigate the anniversary, I went online to make sure everything was okay for the release on the 11th—that was the planned release date for both print and e-book.

Imagine my shock when I realized that the book had been released in e-book format just a few hours before!

Neither the publisher nor Amazon could explain why the system had suddenly kicked into overdrive and released it two days early—but I knew. Sam needed to move the date so October 9th was no longer just the anniversary of his death, but now the anniversary of my first book being published. He was so integral to my becoming a published author that it actually made perfect sense.

That rainbow at Twiddle was the beginning of me understanding that the love Sam shared with the world has been given back to us more than we can explain. Even with his death due to an overdose, with few exceptions, we have not been afflicted with the stigma so many families feel in such a situation. We have been shown love in all sorts of ways, even when we, okay, when *I* wasn't acting in a very lovable manner. We have been encouraged to speak the truth about how he died, and to talk about the huge flaws in our national mental health system. We have found healing and some peace through our working the land, listening to great music, and through remembering to look for those things/people for whom we can be thankful. And through it all, the people Sam met continue to speak his name with love, joy and laughter. To quote Twiddle one more time from their song "White Light":

> *The great white light that burns for us.*
> *It leads us on, it makes us trust.*
> *It shows us love, and drips with pain.*
> *Allows us all to feel the word,*
> *Allows us all to make a change*
> *I can see your light—this is my gift*
> *So many people burning down*
> *So many people need a lift*
> *It starts with one big smile*
> *And grows with every laugh*
> *With every hug and kiss and high-five*
> *Keeps the light from holding back.*

After that concert, I thought a lot about two pieces Sam's friends wrote about him.

The impact that knowing and loving Sam has on my life is ongoing. Of course, his big, open, beautiful heart, his sense of humor and silliness and infectious grin, his creativity and intelligence, his childlike zeal for life and the feeling of belonging he gave to everyone made his soul a special one to me. But in addition to that, Sam had the special impact on my life of acceptance: he was the only friend I had that I could talk to about my father's struggles with alcoholism. He was the only person that understood my mother's neurotic behavior, and loved her and cared about her and wanted to spend time with both of us even though times at my house were dysfunctional at best most of the time. He never, ever judged. That made him so very special, people can say they are without judgment but few actually practice that. I carry an aspiration to one day have that attitude all of the time, and I hope to have that same impact of acceptance on others. Every day I think of Sam at some point in some way. I'm still deeply sad that he is gone, it's a hole in my heart that I don't think time will ever heal. But after the initial wave of sadness subsides, I'm always left with something to think of fondly and smile about, and I feel his presence powerfully in those moments. He's in every sunny day, every verse of a Pink Floyd or Eminem song that comes across the radio waves, and every good time surrounded by friends and laughter. His light is everywhere.

Another friend wrote:

Sam burned his way into my heart and soul, in the most beautiful ways. He was a man of many mysteries, but he was never one for subtlety. I was in awe of his attitude from the start. I didn't understand how someone so strange, so unique, and so dangerously spontaneous could also be so gentle, and passionately kind. Sam made me want to be a more confident person. He constantly encouraged me to see myself the way he saw me; so strange, so unique, so dangerously over prepared— and he showed me how to own my identity. His light made mine want to burn brighter. He did more for me than he could even know, no matter how many times I tried to tell him. For me, this is the core of Sam's legacy. Love as loudly as you yell. Breathe, and get over it. Someone, somewhere, needs us to be stronger and better for them, because they may not have a Frankie Slamcoeur to turn to when the going gets rough.

Reading these messages reminds me that that was Sam's gift to me, to us as a family, to his friends, and hopefully to others—Sam had a light, the light of love, in him that burned so brightly, and the gift of being able to see the light in others. He kept others from holding that light back, bringing their light into the world.

The final words of that song "White Light"? I have them engraved in a bracelet that I wear every day because to me, truer words have never been written.

So many good things come to those who love relentlessly.

My Advice

Years have now passed. As I write this now, I am heading toward the dreaded five-year anniversary. I am about to start my firsts of the five-year markers, and I admit that even thinking about it makes me feel anxious.

What have I learned? I would divide what I have learned into two categories: for those who are not the parents/siblings/grandparents of a child who has died, and for those who are.

First, for those who are lucky enough to have never experienced such a loss and are fortunate enough to still have their child/sibling/grandchild with them, here are some of my personal requests/recommendations:

- There are certain things you should never, ever say under any circumstances, even if you actually believe them. Those things? "He's in a better place." Or, "There's a reason for everything." Or, "God must have needed him/her more than you do." Or, the best: "At least you have your other children." Stop and think for a moment about your words. Is there ever a better place for someone you love than with those who love them? What possible reason could there be for a child to die? If we truly believe God is everywhere, why does God need to take this child away? And finally, the "at least" comment—think about which of your children you would be willing to give up, and just keep the rest.

- Don't give marital advice. While the statistics don't bear out the urban myth that most marriages end in divorce after a child dies, still, the last thing a couple needs to hear is, "You know, most marriages end in divorce after a child dies. I just thought you should know." Nope, not helpful.

- Say the person's name. Say it loud, say it clear, say it with joy and love. Have a great memory of that person? Share it. A picture? Share it. Tons of well-meaning people tell us that they don't mention Sam because they don't want to open that wound again. Truthfully, that wound is always open and festering. Saying his name and sharing a good memory—that is a gift that helps with healing and brings moments of joy.

- Help. Offer to help. Could you offer to bake a batch of cookies for the school bake sale that you know is coming up? Could you take care of the cat when they go away for a night?

- Remember the dates, both the good and the sad. The deceased's birthday? Great time to say, "I'm thinking of him today." The anniversary? "I'm thinking of you all today."

- Food, water, Kleenex, good hand/face cream. If you know someone who is in the early stages of grief, make sure they eat, keep hydrated, and bring them soft tissues. A good friend bought me really good hand/face cream because I was crying so much my nose was raw. Small gestures mean the world.

- Don't push your own views, whether religious or otherwise, on the families.

- If you don't know something for certain, don't gossip. Well, actually, don't gossip at all. But sharing "information" when you don't really know what you are talking about can cause incredible heartburn and heartbreak. For us? There was a rumor that Sam had committed suicide, and many well-meaning people shared that, causing pain and anger all around.

- Know that this person you love will never be the same again after suffering such a loss, and don't try to force them to be something they no longer are. Instead, if you can, embrace the new in them.

- You may not understand why they do certain things, but don't judge. I have a friend who lost one of her daughters. After her daughter's death, she made this incredibly beautiful and intricate flower garden in her honor. Before Sam's death? I admit I thought it was weird. After Sam's death? I am ashamed of my snarky comments about why someone would do something like that. Instead, I wish I had offered to help with the mulching or something. If you can, embrace the things that now mean so much to your friend, and see how you can help.

- Know that you will get it wrong some days, and that's okay. Some days my really well-meaning friends "step in it," but we can all still go forward.

- Remember that love is all that really matters, and to love the people around you relentlessly.

What I would tell another parent/sibling/grandparent in this unfathomable situation?

- You are loved. You loved (and will always love) your child who has died, and that child still loves you. Love doesn't die when the heart stops beating; it is an infinite energy force and it continues. You just need to allow yourself to feel and acknowledge it.

- No one, *no one,* not even your spouse or co-parent, has the right to tell you the right or wrong way to grieve. Your journey belongs to you alone, and whatever you need to do to survive and be healthy should be honored and respected.

- The first of everything—the first birthday, Christmas, etc.—after your child dies is awful. Just plain awful. You may find moments of peace and joy and love, but the hole their loss leaves is so huge that "event" days will never be the same. The good news is that you will get through the firsts, and the fear of them is worse than the actuality. The bad news, for me and for everyone I've asked, is that the second of each of those days is WAY worse than the first. Then, the third and fourth seem a little easier to survive, but I hear (and dread) the fifth, and all the "big" numbers after, are harder again. Accept that you will never have a Mother's Day, Father's Day, Thanksgiving, Christmas, Easter, whatever you celebrate, again that will be as emotionally simple as the ones prior to your loved one's death.

- Family doesn't have to be blood. It is the love that matters.

- You will have to figure out family relationships based on your new reality. Some will be easy to adapt to, others won't.

- Friends who you thought would always be there for you, won't. But new ones will come forward.

- The strangest things will drive you to your knees, howling, keening, rocking in grief. You won't always be able to figure out why something hits you the way it does. There also will be times when you expect this to happen, and it won't.

- Things that once mattered won't, and new things will become really important to you. Don't fight it—embrace it.

- You need to take care of yourself. Eat carefully, drink water, exercise, practice yoga, meditate, do things that are good for your body because that will also help your soul—all important things.

- Allow yourself to feel. Don't try to keep the emotions inside. Some days just let yourself feel the pain, and other days, it's okay to let yourself not feel anything at all, or just curl up for a bit.

- Find hobbies or vocations that can feed your soul. For me, working the soil, seeing food grow and nourish us helped me find my center again, and when I falter, working in the garden helps me find my peace again.

- Listen to your body! There will be times when your mind may not understand something consciously, but your body will show the physical signs of your grief—listen to them and work them through.

- Find the best general medical practitioner you can. You need to have someone who can help keep your body healthy and can also make sure you are taking care of your mental health needs.

- Seek professional help if the darkness is too deep. Your loved one does not want the world to lose you too!

- When people ask what they can do to help, they *usually* mean it, and they want to help. Let them. Would it help if someone made a pan of brownies for your kid's class party, and you aren't able for whatever reason to do it? Someone asks if they can help? Ask them to make the brownies. People love you and they want to help. Give them the gift of *letting* them do so.

- If you want to punch someone who says, "He's in a better place," or "God must have needed him more than you did," or garbage like that—know that a lot of grieving parents will show up to bail you out, I promise. Just kidding, sort of. Walk away when people make such comments—don't engage. Truly, they are trying to be helpful and kind, but they just haven't lived the reality. Vent to one of your "safe people" if you need to; don't let it fester inside of you.

- Find the people in your life who can be your "safe" people. I don't mean the people with whom you share the grief journey completely (such as your co-parent). Instead, I mean people with whom you can let your protective walls down for a bit, who will shield you if needed, and then help you get moving again.

- While you are broken, it doesn't mean you have been destroyed. Think of either the beauty of sea glass or the Japanese pottery repaired with gold—broken, but still strong and beautiful, and even more unique.

- Joy will return. Laughter will return. One day you will think of your child and your first reaction will be to smile, not cry.

- All that love inside you with nowhere to go because you have lost someone you love so much? Turn that love out to the world, and love as fiercely and relentlessly as you can.

———

As time goes on, love changes and shifts, but doesn't lessen. Sam's love is still all around us, guiding us and supporting us. We see his love in how the people he influenced treat each other, how they strive to make the world a better place.

For me, I am Sam's mom. I always will be. At first, I struggled with how to answer the question, "How many children do you have?" I would stand, and then stammer, "Three; no, four. Four, but our son died." Now, I don't stammer. I have four children. I will always have four. One has gone on before me, but I am still his mom; I still strive to protect and love him every single day. And at the end of the day, if I can look myself in the eye and tell myself that I have treated people with the openness he did, I have succeeded, and maybe, just maybe, I am making him proud.

To quote Twiddle one more time: *"When it's time to shut your eyes, inside there's light that gives me life, too blind to see, so pure, so free, the love you gave to those in need, well I'm here my friend, this love won't end I'll spread your word, no I won't turn back when times cut short and all that's left is your sweet love."*—Hattie's Jam

My job is to make sure that Sam's love doesn't end.

What Can You Do?

As I wrote in the prologue, in the end, I wrote this book to hopefully motivate others toward the ideas of recognizing gratitude, connecting with nature, and loving unconditionally. Now, as you think about my journey, I hope you can take time to deliberately recognize the people and things you are thankful for each and every day, and let them know about it. Second, I hope that you will find a way to help yourself through growing something or taking care of the Earth and nature in some way. For me, I don't have any interest in growing flowers, but I love to see my vegetable garden grow. Regardless, growing things helps everything from the air we breathe to our very souls. Finally, I ask you to think about the people in your lives. We all have people that are really easy to love, and it's easy to show that love to them. We all also have people that rub us the wrong way, or those we may shy away from due to our implicit bias. Don't. Find a way to connect. Maybe at first it's just making eye contact in the grocery store, or holding the door for someone. Maybe later it's stopping to say hello to "the weird neighbor" while you're out walking. Start small, stay consistent, and see how you can connect with others.

Many, many chapters ago, I wrote about the scarf I made so many times after Sam's death. That was the scarf where at first I just kept telling Sam I loved him. It was my mantra of love for him. Over time, I started focusing on the intended recipient, and with every stitch, I put my entire heart into showing my love. Very creatively, I call it my "I Love You Scarf."

If you are a knitter (or know one), here is the pattern: with bulky or super bulky yarn, with the appropriate size of circular needle (20 or less), cast on 53 stitches. Knit in the round for four rounds, placing a marker to show the start of a round. Then, knit 3, purl 3, and keep going until the scarf is as deep as you want it to be, then knit 4 more rounds and cast off.

Why did I include the knitting pattern here? I made scarves for so many women who supported us, but then after I made scarves for all these people, I still needed to keep knitting to keep sane. So I started knitting scarves for the local homeless shelters and for the local LGBT teen center. By then, I wasn't knitting them for anyone in particular, but I was still putting love into each one, and dropping bags of them off to be given to those in need helped me feel connected to the rest of humanity.

Find what works for you, show your love to those around you, and love as relentlessly as you can. *That* is my call to action.

Thanks to those who have supported us on this journey

Hopefully this entire book is an acknowledgment of the incredible people in our lives, but I wanted to acknowledge some people directly.

To my amazing editors, Cyn and Sutton—thank you for your editing, and your support as you pushed me to make this book the best it could be. To Morgan James Publishing—thank you for your belief in this project.

To my parents, thank you for your constant love and support even in your own grief. To Ron and Claire, thank you for your support even as you grieved Sam's loss in a new-ish community. To Lynne and Jim—thank you for being there, for phone calls, and for checking on us regularly. To Sean—thank you for showing your love in your tattoo. To Uncle Bob and Aunt Pauline, thank you for saying Sam's name with a smile even when you had tears in your eyes.

To Bamby, thank you for bringing us meals including a salad, crying with us, continuing to say Sam's name, and for leaving the can of SPAM. To Ashton—thank you for keeping Sam up to date on Ben's life, for visiting us, and for your Facebook posts to us.

To Nancy—you were the first fellow grief mother to reach out your hand, and you have never wavered in your support and understanding. I am sure that Sarah and Sam chat regularly about us. To Joanne and Joanie—as the fellow mothers of the young dead in the front row of the Brookside Cemetery, you support us in so many ways, and we thank you for always checking on Sam's spot to make sure it's okay.

To Isabelle, thank you for helping us find our new normal, and for never treating us like we were/are crazy.

To Gary S., thank you for helping make the logistics as easy as possible, and thank you for cleaning Sam's stone.

To Kathy D., thank you for telling me the truth, no matter how much it hurt you to say it and hurt me to hear it.

To Coach M., thank you for your support of Ben even as you grieved yourself.

To the Boston Red Sox, especially David Ortiz and Dustin Pedroia—thank you for winning the 2013 World Series. It was a gift that kept us distracted when we needed it most.

To Twiddle, thanks for making music that brought Sam joy, and has helped us all on this journey. To Kevin R., thanks for helping with the logistics for this book.

To Arlo Guthrie, thanks for decades of music that has made us laugh, cry, think, and bond.

To Vicki and Jon, who say Sam's name with a smile, listen to *Por ti Volare*, and leave hockey items. To Nancy and Gail, thanks for making us feel safe and loved.

To Seth, Michaela, Kim and Mike—Sam was right; you are amazing. Thank you for being our neighbors and our friends.

To Melissa—thanks for always being there for all of us.

To Cheryl—thanks for the check-in texts, the visits, and the constant support.

To Emily N, Taylor, and Hannah K, thank you for being part of our journey. Your memories of Sam bring us joy and peace.

To Zach, thank you for Sam's song, and for singing it with such love.

To Allie, thank you for phone calls, visits, the photos and trees. Your ability to so freely be yourself is an inspiration to us. Thank you also for giving us the cover of this book.

To Leah, thank you for being part of the journey, for remembering Sam with a smile, and for sharing Linnea with us.

To Meredith, Larry, Jim, Michael D, Jeff and Anita, and so many others at Otter Valley—for your constant support of us as a family, and your protection of Ben, your memories of Sam and their celebration of him were so important to us all. To Ray—thank you for proudly speaking of your relationship with Sam to the Otter Valley community.

To the LCS family—thanks for loving all of us, honoring and remembering Sam, and protecting Mormor.

To Muffie—you cried with us then; cry with us still. You took care of Ben at soccer and you loudly remind of us of the love Sam shared with the world, thank you. To Barron and Bronson, thanks for being part of our journey.

To Wil—you never made me feel like I wasn't doing my job; you just sat quietly with me. Thank you. To Mary and Rob, thank you for your love, support, sticky notes, and belief in me when I couldn't believe in myself. To Sally—you brought dark chocolate, said Sam's name, and never told me to cheer up. Thank you.

To Patty and Amy and Laura—you protected me day in and day out for two years, held my hand, handed me Kleenex, cheered me on, and made sure I remembered to eat and drink. I do not think I could have survived at work without you.

To Marc, Pauline, and Nate and Caroline—you had the guts to invite us to go on a trip with you less than two months after Sam's death, you say his name, and you are always there as constant supporters. Thank you for never making us feel like we need to pretend we're okay.

To Avery—thank you for the trees, Twiddle tickets and tears. To Emily H.—thank you for forgiving me for being so cold to you, thank you for your love, and for commenting on how much Sora has Sam's eyes. To Kirsten—thank you for posting music, memories, and photos. To Cody—you tell us you love us regularly and loudly, you visit Sam often, and you never forget the joy and love. Thank you. To Zaccheus and Kaitlyn—thank you for your love and support, and for Sammy. To Arlie—thank you for doing laundry, making a bag from Sam's clothes, and for your expression of how much Sam's love meant to you. To Hannah, John, and Harper—you brought the garlic, loved Sam, bring joy and memories, and gave us Asa Samuel. Thank you.

To Bernadette and Garrett—thank you for your love, laughter, cookies, a baby blanket, and constant support. To Will and Maureen—you visit, bake, say Sam's name with joy and love, check on Ben, and help us remember the good times. Thank you. To Dot and Royadon—you checked on us all, and you helped us remember the stupid silly (and not so silly) times too.

To Lyndsay—you Twiddle with us, visit, text, remember us on Mother's Day and Father's Day, and just keep Sam's love alive. Thank you for always being there.

To Amie—through the loss, you also had to learn to be a first-time mom to the most amazing of little girls, and then adjust to being the mom to twins too. Your ability to juggle and keep going shows your incredible inherent strength.

To Sora—you are amazing, and I am so proud to be your grandma. Your Uncle Sam looks down on you with pride, joy, and love.

To Ed—you got on the first flight out here, fed us, drove us, kept us hydrated, made us laugh, protected my parents, and reminded us of the need to keep going. Your humor keeps me grounded, and I can't imagine a better big brother figure.

To Linnea—your constant, unflinching, loud, loyal support means more than I can say, and I am so thankful for your ability to simultaneously hold my hand and kick me in the behind.

To Ryan—you had to fight your own demons while grieving your best friend. Your decision to find the right path and then following it is an inspiration to us all. Thank you for your unending support of this book, and for letting me feed you even now. I can't express how thankful I am to have you in my/our life, and how proud I am to call you my son.

To Ben—you had to grow up overnight, lost your best friend, had to navigate adolescence, grief, and struggling parents all at the same time. Your humor and patience, with my constant text messages and my need to know you are okay, mean so much. Your strength, patience, courage, and support are a constant joy, and I'm so thankful that I am your mom.

To Paul—I do not know how anyone can survive this pain without a partner who understands what the other is going through. Your grace, love, honesty, transparency, strength, and courage inspire me daily. You are my best friend and the love of my life. Thank you for never telling me to cheer up, never questioning my strange ways of dealing with grief, never minimizing our pain. Thank you also for being my loudest cheerleader on this writing journey.

About the Author

Kris Francoeur, writer and educator, is a grieving mother who has found joy and light again through the practices of conscious and deliberate gratitude, unconditional acceptance, and connection with nature. Born in Massachusetts, then having moved around for her first years in Massachusetts and New Jersey, she moved to Vermont with her parents, and completed her schooling there. With master's degrees in both counseling psychology and educational leadership, Kris writes with authority about grief and moving forward in our very busy and stressful world. A published author of fiction, Kris has published three romance novels (*More Than I Can Say*, *That One Small Omission*, and *The Phone Call*) with Solstice Publishing using her pen name, Anna Belle Rose. She lives in beautiful Addison County, Vermont, with her husband and youngest son, a small herd of alpacas, a flock of chickens and several hives of bees. Kris loves to spend time with her extended family, spending time in the garden and spinning the alpaca fiber into yarn.

———

Want to connect with Kris?

Webpage: www.authorkfrancoeur.com

Twitter: @KFAnnaBelleRose

Facebook: www.facebook.com/authorkfrancoeur

Morgan James makes all of our titles available
through the Library for All Charity Organization.

www.LibraryForAll.org

CPSIA information can be obtained
at www.ICGtesting.com
Printed in the USA
LVHW092100251121
704454LV00007B/1044

9 781642 791815